# THE COMPLETE BOOK OF BASEBALL CARDS

## By Steve Clark

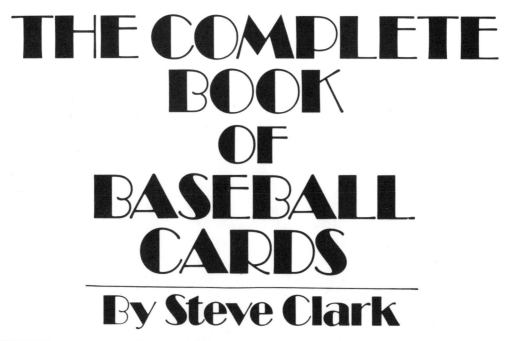

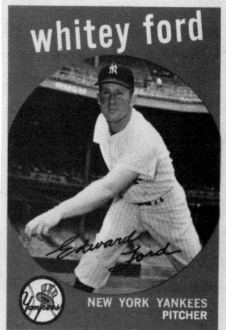

## Foreword by Paul Gallico

An Associated Features Book

GROSSET & DUNLAP, INC.
A Filmways Company
Publishers • New York

I would like to thank several people who played a large role in making this book a reality: Zander Hollander of Associated Features, who originated the idea and sold the book; collectors Woody Gelman, Wayne Varner, the late Tommy Holmes, and others who shared their knowledge with me; members of the New York Mets and Chicago Cubs who shared some memories; Sy Berger and his staff at Topps Chewing Gum; and the employees of the Prints Department at the Metropolitan Museum of Art. Special thanks must be given to Norman Liss and Steve Schwartz, who stepped out of their roles as public relations men to provide real enthusiasm and friendship. And to Bob Rathgeber of the Cincinnati Reds, for making available some of the cards that appear in the book.

*Steve Clark*
Larchmont, New York

To my brothers and old "flipping" buddies,
Paul and Peter,
and to sister Kathy,
who came along after the cards
had been put away.

# Foreword

LAJOIE, CLEVELAND

| | |
|---|---|
| Christy Mathewson | Ed Walsh |
| Cy Young | Joe McGinnity |
| Three-Finger Brown | Wild Bill Donovan |
| Honus Wagner | Hughie Jennings |
| Rube Waddell | Eddie Collins |
| Home Run Baker | Ed Delahanty |
| Roger Bresnahan | Ernie Shore |
| Fred Merkle | Smokey Joe Wood |
| Nap Lajoie | Buck Herzog |
| Amos Rusie | George Sisler |
| Ty Cobb | Tris Speaker |
| Tinker-Evers-Chance | Zack Wheat |

Does that list of names shown here — or *any one* included — mean anything to you? If you are a dyed-in-the-wool baseball fan with a love of the game that has taken you into its past, you will recognize many of them. But if you are of this generation, interested only in your home team, their rivals, and the well-known players of the augmented leagues of today, these players will be strangers to you.

In any case, if you possessed a set of cards measuring about an inch and a half by two and a half inches that would fit, say, inside a pack of ordinary cigarettes — and including, besides many other baseball stars, the galaxy listed — you would be on the way toward becoming a millionaire. For those baseball cards of my youth, which I used to collect more than 60 years ago, between the ages of 10 and 14, had I hung onto them, would be worth a fortune today. My memories of them are tender and fond. Like all kids my age, I collected, hoarded, traded, and did business with them. This book will tell you the fas--cinating story of their origin and development.

My own memory is naturally not to be relied upon. Where did the cards come from? — how did I get them? — these gaudy, olio reproductions of the baseball heroes and giants of my youth.

I would venture two sources. Bought or begged. The cards came inserted into each pack of Sweet Caporal cigarettes, a "coffin nail" popular in those days. Naturally, at the tender age mentioned, I had nothing to do with the smoke, but one could cadge the cards from one's elders.

My recollection, too, is that they were packaged with various brands of bubble gum and a slab of rock-like toffee.

The toffee cards were more diverse and included representations of Bleriot's monoplane, the Wright Brothers' first glider, James Watts' steam engine, and, if you were lucky, a ballplayer.

All of the above paragraphs may be the garbled pseudo-memories of an old gent. But the fact remains that I once owned all of those baseball cards of some of the greatest players the sport has ever known, which includes right up to today, and that I cherished them.

I suppose a lot of latter-day successful businessmen got their start by wheeling and dealing with baseball cards. We often kept two packets held together by rubber bands, one being our major collection, and the other one being duplicates for trading. In the trading market, of course, you had to know your baseball, fielding, pitching, batting averages, and general ability. No kid would be foolish enough to swap a .200 hitter for a player nudging the .300 mark, or exchange a pitcher whose strikeout record was anemic compared to that of another. I would say that in this manner the youth of my day absorbed something of market values in the operation of the economic system. And if they could manage, in the form of cards of baseball heroes, to buy low and sell high (finding a sucker who didn't know as much as they did about averages), they'd prosper later in life, too.

There was also a form of gambling with them, akin to marbles, in which a skilled operator could, in a few minutes before the school bell rang for the first class, denude you of some of your most precious possessions.

I might intrude here the memory that you didn't always pull a star out of every purchased packet. There were a large number of clucks in evidence. If each cigarette pack, bubble gum pack, or candy bar had included some supernova, everybody would have possessed them and the market for the product would have dwindled. So you kept on buying in the hope of hitting a Christy Mathewson or a Home Run Baker. It was for this reason that when you got your hands on a real good prize, you guarded it.

One of the gambling games was called "Flipping the Cards," and for the life of me I cannot remember today how it was played, but you'll find it in Steve Clark's research into the long-ago. What I do remember is that invariably I wound up the loser. Whatever "flipping" was, I was rotten at it.

But I can see myself outside P.S. 6, which was then at the corner of Madison

Avenue and 86th Street, entering the little candy store glued to one end of the school like a small parasite and caught up in the excitement of buying a couple of jawbreakers to see what colored card would be enclosed and whose likeness would be on it. I was an addict to this collector's craze, but I also worshipped the players depicted. You will be amused today at how they looked in the uniforms they wore. To us, though, they were greater than kings, emperors or presidents.

After school I played stickball or One Ol' Cat in the streets, and when I managed – to get a hit, it wasn't me but old Honus Wagner driving the ball out of the park. I hadn't the slightest inkling that I would grow up one day to begin professional life as chronicler of the doings of the baseball greats of my adult days — Babe Ruth, Lou Gehrig, Ted Williams, and the rest of the heroes of the golden decades of the Twenties and Thirties.

Never mind — here is a book rich in retrospect and valuable in romance. Enjoy it as I have. And I understand that the baseball cards are bigger than ever. Hang onto them, kids! I wish I had kept mine!

*Paul Gallico*
Antibes
1976

# Contents

# 1
# Baseball Cards—
# Yesterday and Today

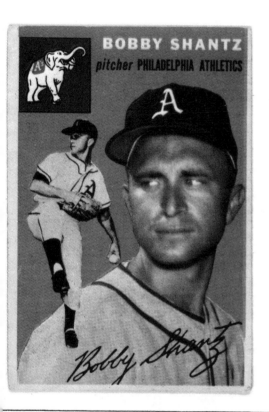

To paraphrase Henry Wadsworth Longfellow's famous poem: "Hardly a man is now alive who remembers the day when there were no baseball cards."

Baseball and other sports cards made their debut in the 1880's when they were included in tobacco and cigarette pouches. Later, after the first World War, candy companies jumped on the baseball-card bandwagon. Then, beginning in the 1930's, gum manufacturers began producing the cards. Intermittently, through the years, regional companies (usually local food manufacturers) included them with their products.

Today, except for several independent card manufacturers of little significance outside collecting circles, Topps Chewing Gum, Inc. means baseball cards. On every 15-cent, 25-cent, and "three-pack" package of cards sold at the local candy store, there is the ever-present mark of Topps, a red "T" that seems to be smiling, trailed by the "opps."

The birth of card manufacturing can be traced to two inventions that came into

Billy Wilson    PITCHER

"RED" RUFFING

wide use in America during the 1860's and 1870's.

Lithography, the process by which printed or photographic material is reproduced in large quantities, was invented in 1798 by a German named Aloys Senefelder. In the early 19th century many of Europe's great artists used it to reproduce their drawings.

In the late 1830's, photography began to be used with this printing process. Earlier, photographs had been pasted on cardboard for distribution. By the 1860's, lithography was in wide commercial use in America. It remained the most popular method of color reproduction for the remainder of the 19th century.

Sometime in the early 1870's, workers at the Duke Cigarette Company in North Carolina found a way to package cigarettes cheaply. The notion of fitting little cards into these packages came into being shortly thereafter and a number of other companies soon followed suit.

In his pamphlet, *Baseball Cards: Everything You Always Wanted to Know, But Didn't Know Who to Ask*, baseball card collector and historian Gar Miller breaks down the history of the baseball card into five periods.

The first period is from 1886 to 1900. The photographs of the players were stilted studio poses printed on handsome sepia paper. Cameras shot away at ballplayers apparently swinging at a ball which was suspended from a string or as they slid on a carpet. The tremendous charge of flash powder used in photography to provide lighting in those days often gave the players a "pop-eyed" expression.

All of the cards were included free of charge in tobacco or cigarette pouches, but they were, of course, difficult for youngsters and non-smokers to obtain. Old Judge Cigarettes were most likely the first to issue pictures of baseball players with the product. Two other companies — Mayo, and Allen and Ginter — then followed suit.

Miller's second period ranges from 1908 to 1915, when many tobacco companies began to manufacture their own baseball cards, along with other cards. Some of the companies, besides portraying major-leaguers, pictured minor-league players as well.

Non-tobacco companies also got into the act during this period. Sporting Life Newspapers, Tip-Top Bread, and Cracker Jacks (which ran a series called "Cracker Jack Players") were in this group.

The period from 1916 to 1932 is considered a relatively quiet time in the distribution of baseball cards, according to Miller. Few cards from these days exist today, probably because of the questionable quality of the cards. Some of them were sold by anonymous manufacturers in strips of ten (as opposed to companies which included cards free with their product). Caramel candy companies began to produce a larger size (2" by 3") black-and-white card.

The fourth period, 1933 to 1941, was highlighted by the advent of the bubble gum card. Paving the way was the Goudey Company of Boston. Goudey was followed by the DeLong Company of Boston and the National Chicle Company of Philadelphia. According to Miller, a theory exists that "because of the many paper drives that were conducted in the 1930's — a depression recovery period — an overwhelming majority of those cards issued were discarded. They are, for the most part, more difficult to find than cards from the early 1900's."

Miller's final period is from 1948 to the present. After a seven-year gap that included World War II, when no cards were manufactured, the modern era in baseball-card collecting began. Most of the cards, until 1955, were issued by Leaf and Bowman. Fleers of Philadelphia distributed special series cards—All-Time Greats, Ted Williams cards in the late 1950's and early 1960's — but never went "wholesale" into the baseball-card business. Regional companies, such as Glendale Meats, Hunter's Wieners, Red Heart Dog Food, Bell Brand Chips, and Johnston Cookies, also issued cards on baseball players during this period.

Topps came out with its first complete series of individual baseball players in 1951 (although it had pictured a few baseball stars in its 1949 "Hocus Focus" series). At that time, Bowman, another gum company, was monopolizing the industry. But in 1952 Topps came out with a prototype card (2½″ by 3½″) which included statistics, emblems, signatures, and player histories. Within four years, Bowman was out of business.

In the years since, Topps has improved and diversified its cards with more sophisticated techniques and imagination. In addition to individual player cards, Topps annually puts out All-Star cards, Rookie All-Star cards, Team Rookie cards, Leader cards, Playoff and World Series cards, and Team cards. The company also offers new gimmicks every year — MVP series cards. Sporting News cards, Boyhood All-Star cards, Father-Son cards, traded cards, and other combination cards.

It all appears to have worked, for according to company figures, Topps sells an estimated 250,000,000 cards every year. Baseball cards have enabled the manufacturers of Bazooka, Gold Rush, Big Buddy, Garbage Candy, and Big Tooth to experience growth of about one hundred percent in the last decade.

With all this success, Topps has been able to purchase two "homes," one in the Bush Terminal area of Brooklyn, New York, where the creative, marketing and sports divisions are located, and one in the country, in Duryea, Pennsylvania, where the cards and gum are manufactured.

Topps Sports Director Seymour ("Sy") Berger has been with the sports operation from the very beginning. At his Brooklyn office, with baseball mementos scattered all about, Sy Berger related Topps' early roller-coaster days. (After all, renowned Coney Island is only a few miles away.)

"When Topps put out its 1951 series," Berger says, "we were neophytes. We made certain errors that inexperienced people make. Twenty-five years ago, we had nothing — just an idea and a list of players' names. I was in sales and head of the Sports Department, too. I used to write all the copy for the baseball cards at home on weekends. You don't know what it's like to think of something nice to write about a guy who hits .195. I mean, what can you say — 'This guy stinks'?"

Topps learned fast, though. With an improved card in 1952 and well-researched statistics and player histories (taken from up-to-date files of sports magazines, newspapers, club publications and TV/radio guides), Topps eventually purchased part of Bowman and began its virtual baseball-card monopoly at the tender age of five.

On the second floor of Topps' Brooklyn building, 25 years of Topps cards are pasted inside bulging albums. In these books are the pictures of thousands of men who played baseball — some who have become successful businessmen in years hence; some who coach today; rookies with great promise who made it big in baseball, others who never made it onto a second baseball card.

In the 1953 cards, a painted stadium is in the background and a Red Sox with a bat, or an elephant, or a cub, or two cardinals on a bat, or a one-eyed pirate, is to the left of an earlier major-leaguer named

Big Luke, Big George, Peanuts, Country, or Ozark Ike. On the reverse side, with his statistics, are questions like: "Who is called a Bill Klem in baseball?" (He is someone who is never wrong; Klem was considered one of the best umpires.) Or, "What was the weight of the first official baseball?" (5½ to 6 ounces.)

"Many baseball experts say that switch-hitting Mickey is the greatest baseball prospect ever seen," reads the blurb on Mickey Mantle's card. It doesn't say quite as much on the cards of Dick Bokelman, Forrest Main, Morris Martin, Freddie Marsh, and Bob Olds.

In 1954 there was an "Inside Baseball" series on the back of each card. "Hank [Sauer] was the fans' choice for the 1950 All-Star Game (an illustration showing Sauer's name being written into the line-up). The NL mgr. didn't want to use him (picture of a manager). But in '52 Hank silenced his critics by smashing a two-run HR, beating the AL Stars 3-2!" Ted Kluzewski's wife, according to his card, took pictures of his swing after a poor year, and after Big Klu studied the films during the off-season, he improved his .259 batting average to .320. Ferris Fain found a bat left by a group of kids playing ball. With this bat, the card noted, he won the batting championship.

A year later, Topps had Double Header cards. There was, for example, a likeness of Al Kaline swinging from his shoes when the card was open, and Corky Valentine in the middle of his wind-up when the card was folded over.

In 1957, there are simply posed action shots of a Peewee Reese, Sal Maglie, or Warren Spahn, in front of an empty stadium. The backs of the cards had each player's year-by-year statistics. But in 1958, Topps brought back the headshots, team insignia, and illustrations on the back, with only the previous year's (and career) statistics.

In 1959, the player's face was in a circle, with all of his year-by-year statistics on the back. Journeyman John Romonowsky, for instance, has his one year with the Washington Senators positioned at the very bottom of his statistics from twelve years in the minors. There were special cards like Batter Bafflers, Tom Brewer and Dick Sisler; Words of Wisdom, Casey Stengel and Don Larsen; Buck Hill Aces, Ron Kline, Bob Friend, Vernon Law and Elroy Face. Team cards have a players' checklist on the back. The first Topps Rookie All-Stars included players like pitcher Jim O'Toole of the Cincinnati Red-

legs and catcher Johnny Romano of the Cleveland Indians.

The 1960 cards had the players' season highlights on the back — if there were any. World Series cards made their first appearance. "Neal steals second in Game No. 1." (But the White Sox won that game, 11-0.) "Champs Celebrate" after the Dodgers ended the Series with champagne shampoos. Batting and home-run and pitching leaders finally got their own card.

Two years later, Topps led off with Roger Maris, who was called "the most discussed player of the decade." In addition, Topps came out with a series called "Baseball Bucks." Mickey Mantle, Roger Maris, Warren Spahn, and Stan Musial had a face value of $10; Roy Sievers, $5; Jerry Lumpe, $1.

With the 1963 cards were All-Time Great Cards — Jack Chesbro, Christy Mathewson, Rogers Hornsby.

There were "magic answers" on the backs of the 1964 cards. (To find an an-

"JOE" CRONIN

WHEAT, BROOKLYN

JACKIE ROBINSON
*third base* BROOKLYN DODGERS

swer, you used a nickel to rub.) There were special stand-up cards. The Yankee manager that year was Yogi Berra, and for his card's picture he didn't shave.

In 1966, there was a move down to waist shots. In 1969, there was the added attraction of "Super baseball" cards — a large headshot with a signature. Scratch-off cards — having spots on the back where, when scratched, the words *strike* or *ball* or *fly out* appeared — came out in 1971. The surprise package in 1972 was the Boyhood Stars — Bud Harrelson in a Little League uniform, Chris Speier in his back-yard. The following years had the "Traded" series, the 25th anniversary cards (picturing the MVPs over the years), and the Father-Son series.

The regular series of 660 cards includes "in-action" pictures from actual game situations — Rico Petrocelli and Deron Johnson connecting, Mike Andrews making the pivot, Thurman Munson getting dirt in his face while tagging out a runner.

You might say that it was a long way from the days when ballplayers on cards were pictured swinging at a ball on a string in a studio.

# 2
# From Topps to You

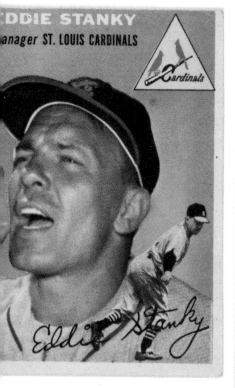

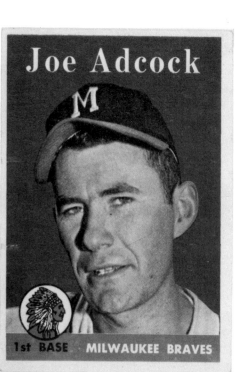

That baseball card of Hank Aaron, Darrel Chaney, Tom Seaver, or Sixto Lezcano has traveled quite a distance before ending up in a back pocket. From the image captured at a ballpark somewhere, it has had stopovers in Brooklyn, New York, and Duryea, Pennsylvania, en route to the candy store.

Topps Chewing Gum employs photographers who pursue ballplayers throughout the season in an attempt to get them to say "cheese" at least several times.

The photographers begin their shooting odyssey in March, during spring training. Topps tries to get as complete a set of photographs as possible during this time. Additional pictures are then taken during the regular season.

"We evaluate the pictures after spring training," says Sy Berger. "From that point on, we fill in during the season for better photographs, new players and those who have been traded. We also reshoot the players who grew mustaches during the year or changed their hair styles.

"We take a minimum of six to eight

shots of every ballplayer. They include head shots, three-quarter length shots, full-length shots, and action shots. We're very fussy over the pictures. Fifty to sixty percent are considered NG [no good] and shot again. We don't have time to take each picture and touch it up."

Running his eyes to an attractive magazine cover of Catfish Hunter on his desk, Berger adds, "Now, this picture we would never use — there's too much shadow."

By and large, the pictures on the Topps baseball cards are quite good. In any case, there is no doubt that the photography has improved a great deal over the years.

"Our photography was not the best in years past," admits Berger. "We had only one part-time photographer. All of the players wound up in similar poses — catchers with their fists clenched, managers with their hands cupped over their mouths yelling out instructions. It was pretty embarrassing.

"Every card until 1971 showed a posed shot. Then we started using action shots, which give a good variety. Our market research shows that youngsters prefer that. We give a variety in our current year's series between action and posed shots. We also attempt to show a different type of picture of each player than the one we had the previous year. After all, we're basically in the children's entertainment business."

For years, more observant youngsters might have wondered why certain players were always shown without caps. Was it accidental? Or did the player just like to show off his butch haircut? Research would disclose that, in every case, a player without a hat was a player with a new team.

In recent years, Topps has discovered a more professional way of handling the problem of the traded ballplayer. "We take several shots from the floor up now," explains Berger. "That's so that the insignia

on the cap is indistinguishable. For example, look at Milt May, traded during an off-season from Pittsburgh to Houston. We simply paint the brim of the hat and the trim around the uniform."

The Topps picture file is a marvel in itself, containing pictures of players from the time of their baseball infancy to their veteran days. The files, of course, come in handy when the company prepares to issue certain "specials." The Most Valuable Player series in 1975, for example, included the original baseball-card pictures of the winners of each year. The 1953 MVPs, solemn-looking Cleveland Indian third baseman Al Rosen and smiling Brooklyn Dodger catcher Roy Campanella, are shown as they looked in their heyday.

Of course, since Topps has been in the business only since 1951, there is the difficulty of finding pictures of some of the older players. It presented a problem for the Father-Son series earmarked for 1976. "I asked outfielder Del Unser if he had any baseball photos of his father, Al [a catcher in the 1940's for the Detroit Tigers and Cincinnati Reds]," says Berger. "Al Unser is a close friend of mine, yet we can't seem to find any of his pictures."

The 1952 card is considered the model for all cards issued since then. It is a giant-sized card with a color picture done by a process called Flexichrome. The front of the card has the team emblem, the player's signature, and heading — name, position, team. The back of the card includes year and lifetime statistics on the player, together with personal data.

Today, once the pictures of the players are processed, they are printed on square sheets of cardboard, 132 to a sheet. The backside information is then stripped onto the cards by people in the art department. They also airbrush the original photographs of the players before they are

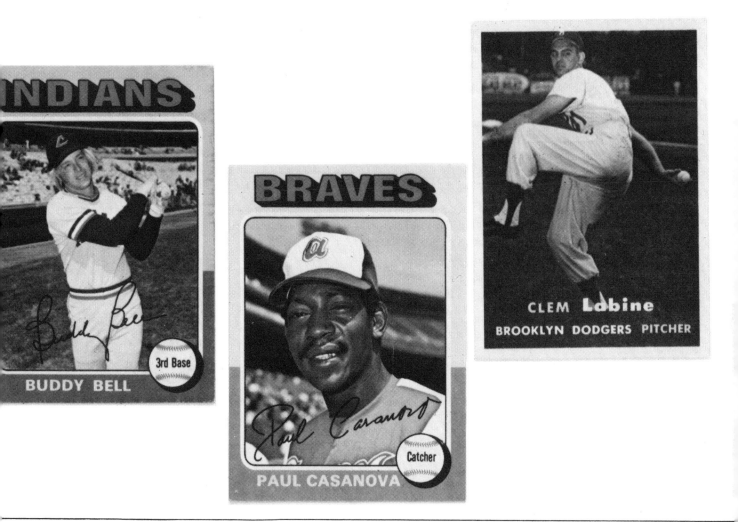

printed. This is done mainly to get rid of certain markings on the uniform of the player who is traded (like the Yankee pinstripe) or to improve the appearance of a player with blemishes. The next procedure, the most important step in the making of the card, next to the photography itself, is cutting and collating the cards, which takes place at the Duryea (Pennsylvania) factory. Special machines mix the cards, so that it is technically impossible (machines, like people, do make mistakes, though) for two Denny Doyles or two Frank Taverases to be found in the same pack.

One of the more important changes Topps has instituted in recent years is the single-series concept. Before 1974, Topps issued five or six series annually, which meant that a group of new faces would appear on cards at the candy store every six weeks or so. This, it was thought, would remedy the recurrence of the same likeness of Tony Kubek or Walt Dropo or Gus Triandos popping up throughout a season.

As Berger told the authors of *The Great American Baseball Card* several years ago before the change: "We sometimes run into backdrops at the distribution point. Say a guy with a small corner store in the Bronx orders twenty cartons of Series One cards. He sells out in three or four weeks, and so he reorders fifteen cartons. By now, the kids in his area have all the Series One cards, so that by the time Series Two is ready for distribution, the storekeeper finds himself with ten cartons of Series One left. So he goes light on Series Two, all the time trying to get rid of his Series One. By the time the fifth or sixth series has come out, he has himself backlogged right up to his eyeballs. It's sort of a snowball effect in reverse."

The problem was especially apparent when it came to sending new-series cards out to the West Coast in the 1950's, where with added mailing time a factor some stores never got the final One or Two series. In fact, collectors today double the price on the higher-series cards of those earlier years.

This problem seems to have been solved by issuing all 660 cards in a single series extending from March to September.

Contrary to popular belief, Topps manufactures the same number of cards annually for each player pictured. In other words, there are as many Mike Marshall and Bobby Bonds cards as there are Doug Flynn and Diego Segui cards. The only concession Topps makes to the stars of the game is to reserve cards ending in "0" or "5" for them. When a notable record has been broken, the player who eclipsed the earlier mark may be given the honor of leading off the Topps series. Roger Maris was duly honored in 1962 after hitting 61 home runs the year before. Hank Aaron was No. 1 in 1974, the year he was scheduled to break Babe Ruth's career home-run mark of 714.

As witnessed, the baseball card begins a slow yearly trek from the spring training camps in Florida and Arizona in March, or from actual ballparks later on in the year, to Topps' Brooklyn offices, where they are prettied up by the art department and affixed to large sheets of cardboard, to Duryea, Pennsylvania, where they are cut and sorted so that there are no duplications in a pack, to a local candy store in Little Rock, Bayonne, or Kansas City, and then to a final resting place in someone's torn pocket or scruffy shoe box.

# 3
# The Players

Memorabilia of the New York Mets is much in evidence as soon as you walk into the Diamond Club at Shea Stadium in Flushing, N.Y. Paintings on the lobby walls depict Met players of today and yesterday. The smiling face of the Met-insignia baseball is everywhere. Real-life players can often be seen relaxing or chatting with friends here as they while away the hours before game time.

The Mets are playing the Chicago Cubs today. Escorting me is Sy Berger, a close friend of many of the big-league players.

"This is Jose Cardenal," Berger says on walking into the Cub locker room. "Jose is like a son to me. I straightened him out

when he was a 17-year old kid . . . Darrold Knowles here is a well-traveled pitcher. He has been around a long time."

Knowles takes exception to the adjective "well-traveled."

"Well, you are!" Berger smiles back.

"Rick Monday," Berger says, patting the Cub outfielder's middle, "it looks like you're gaining some weight."

Berger continues to renew acquaintances with old friends, and introduces himself to some of the younger players. Bill Madlock laughingly tells Berger, "I want my release from Topps for $3,000."

Yet Madlock remembers the delight of being on a baseball card for the first time.

"It was a great thrill to me. It means that you are a major-leaguer. I've never had any complaints about the picture they use.

"I was too poor to collect cards when I was a kid, but my own kids collect them today. They traded their friends twenty cards for me. That's got to make you feel good."

Rick Monday, who played the first part of his career for the Oakland Athletics before being traded to Chicago, can't recall the feelings he had on seeing his own baseball card for the first time. Yet he does remember collecting cards as a kid, hoping

Berger's next stop is the field, where several Met pitchers are engaged in batting practice. Jon Matlack collars Berger to discuss the kind of furniture he has coming for his royalties. Relief pitcher Skip Lockwood wants to know how much compensation from Topps he's entitled to. Jerry Koosman says to Berger, "I want a boat and camper just like Willie [Mays] got."

In the locker room, many of the Mets are autographing baseballs. Berger introduces himself to Mike Vail, a rookie outfielder called up from the minors. He shakes hands with Bud Harrelson, just re-

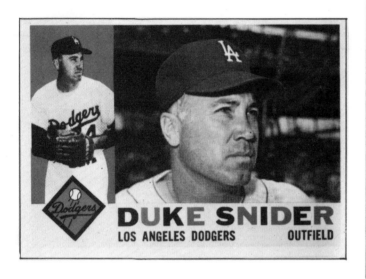

that some day he would have his own picture on one. Today, his own cards turn up at many banquets he attends. "I'll be speaking at a banquet and a kid will come up and show me a baseball card and ask me to autograph it. I'll bet him a Coke that he can't tell me what stadium the picture was shot in."

covered from an operation. "My hero, Bud — how's your knee? . . . I'll see what I can do about getting you on a card for next year."

Topps' Rookie All-Star ballots are being handed out to the clubs today. "Don't vote for your teammates," says Berger. "Can we vote for our teammates?" asks pitcher Rick

Baldwin. While the Cubs filled their ballots out immediately, the Mets are tardy with theirs. "Fill 'em out, fill 'em out," Berger shouts impatiently.

An autographed team picture, with catcher Jerry Grote included, passes by Berger. "This is the last time I saw Grote smile," Berger says. The baseball-card man then asks Jesus Alou how brother Felipe is. "Tell Felipe, when you see him, that he's still my favorite Alou," Berger kids.

Infielder Harrelson remembers his first baseball card. "I was sort of excited. It's something that you always cherish. I had

my pictures the first few years, but they've been better lately — maybe I've gotten better-looking."

First baseman Ed Kranepool became a big-leaguer at the tender age of 17, and his first baseball card came out the following year. "I was on a rookie card with Tony Oliva of the Minnesota Twins and Jimmy Hall of the Cleveland Indians. There was a fourth guy on the card, but I can't remember who." (Kranepool's memory is worse than that. Others on the card that year were Oliva, Max Alvis of the Indians, and Bob Bailey of the Pirates.)

**Boyhood Photos of the Stars**

BOBBY
★ MURCER

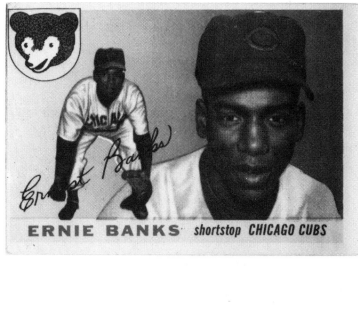

ERNIE BANKS shortstop CHICAGO CUBS

people from all over sending cards to me. Some of the photos of me are not that good — but then, again, you don't have that much to work with," he adds modestly.

Felix Millan, another infielder, has a good reaction to the cards. "I always see kids playing with them, though I never had them as a boy. I wasn't so happy with

"I was also on a card during my second year with Casey Stengel. The card read something like 'Casey Teaches.'

"I've kept one card from each year. Maybe I'll put them all together on a poster or something in a few years. I've seen other guys do it, and it looks real good to me.

"Every year the cards seem to get better. They seem more professional. There were times when they took pictures when I hadn't shaved or had a haircut, and I just didn't look too good. Now, when they come around, I try to make sure I'm ready.

"The cards are great for kids. I used to scale and flip them as a kid. I didn't have the money to buy them, so I won them." Catcher Ron Hodges hasn't forgotten the initial reaction to his first card. "I was proud and amazed to be on a Topps card, and to be a major-leaguer. My family ran out and started buying cards. It took them quite a while before they could find mine. I collected at times as a kid, but I never thought I'd ever appear on one.

"One thing they asked us was what our hobbies were. I put down dancing. I've always gotten a lot of kidding since the card appeared. Guys are always asking me to do a dance for them."

For all of the time, money and care that goes into the production of baseball cards, and for all of the joy a collector or flipper gets from them, the situation would never have come about without the likes of, say, Honus Wagner, Lou Gehrig, Joe DiMaggio, Ted Williams, Tom Seaver, and Cesar Cedeno, to name a few of the thousands of big-league players of the game. There would have been no cards with your tobacco, Grandpa, or with your gum, sonny, without them. The guy whose face is on one side of the card, and whose statistics are on the back, is the essential ingredient.

So what players are pictured? And what does each have to gain?

At Topps, each player who is on a major-league roster for the first 31 days of the season is paid a guaranteed sum of $250. He also shares in the proceeds (a royalty) on sales. Additionally, he receives a bonus of $75 every other year, which brings the total to about $400 annually.

If desired, the ballplayer may accept gifts in lieu of cash. The Topps Gift Catalog includes watches, cameras, furniture, tools, camping gear, typewriters, luggage, etc.

Every ballplayer who enters organized

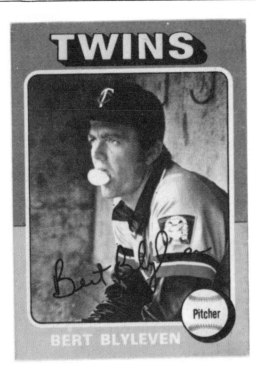

baseball today is signed by Topps. He is given a $5 binder and told to "go buy a steak." According to Sy Berger, this is how the term "steak money" came into being.

Signing ballplayers to card contracts is not what it was before 1960. Today, with Topps as the only thriving major company in the business of producing baseball cards, there is no longer a need to compete with other companies, or for it to be selective in signing players.

In the early 1950's, when Topps first began to compete for the baseball-card clientele with Bowman and Fleers, players generally went with the best offer. "Back then," says Berger, "a fellow by the name of Joe Garagiola looked me right in the eye and told me he had not signed another contract with anyone else. All the time I had his Bowman contract right in my desk. But what a guy!"

Until the late 1950's, a Topps' scout was sent to spring training camps to sign up players likely to make the jump to the big leagues. According to Berger, this policy was changed for "humane reasons."

"We were going through some soul searching at this time. I consider myself a humanist, and it became depressing for me to have our men go into a clubhouse of 25 boys to sign 10 or 12 of them and have the others feel rejected.

"I personally remember going down to an early Chicago Cubs' camp. Bob Scheffing was the manager then and a lot of the team's young players were there. I walked into camp and found out who the better ballplayers were. The players I didn't sign up said they'd like to sign, too, but I refused them, based on the information I had received. Imagine, hearing from a bubble-gum man that you are not going to realize your dream!

"At about the same time, we had our scout, Turk Karam — who once scouted for the Brooklyn Dodgers, New York Yankees, and Chicago Cubs, and who was considered a good judge of talent — go down to the Detroit Tigers' training camp. A young man was there who had been sent over by the Dodgers. His name was Maury Wills. Turk spoke to the Detroit people and

JOHNSON, WASHINGTON

TIGERS

John Hiller   PITCHER

SPARKY LYLE Pitcher

RED SOX

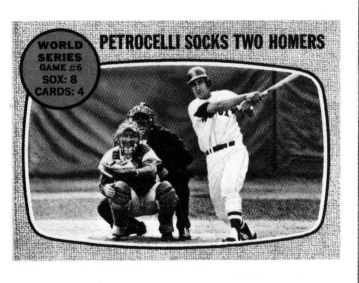

**PETROCELLI SOCKS TWO HOMERS**

WORLD SERIES GAME #6 SOX: 8 CARDS: 4

1954 · **HANK AARON SPECIAL** · 1955
1956 — 1957

watched Maury play. And, based upon what he heard, there was no way that Maury Wills could be a major-league prospect. He had a weak arm and couldn't hit very well. So we didn't sign him. The Tigers missed out, too, of course, by returning him to the Dodgers.

"Afterwards, I remember sending a note to Turk. Wills had been the only one not signed in that Detroit training camp in 1958. I wrote, 'Why hurt the guy's feelings?'

"Maury stayed angry at us for some time, even after he made the majors. He didn't sign with us until about his eighth year with the Dodgers. He was the only major-leaguer we didn't have under contract. You couldn't blame him, of course. After that, we signed every player in the minors and saved ourselves headaches."

To add a nice ending to the Wills' tale, Berger adds, "Maury's one of my closest friends now. A few years ago, he came into town at four o'clock in the morning with-

out any tickets for the World Series. He called me up and asked if I could help him. Of course, I got him the tickets."

Berger and his writers get together before the winter baseball meetings in December to decide who will be immortalized on cardboard in the coming season. "We go about it very scientifically. We look at the team rosters and decide who will make the team.

"We base our decision on the club's needs. You get a kid who hits .340 in the minors, but the team has a good player who plays the same position. Unless there's a trade, or the kid's options are up [a team can lose the rights to a player if he's left too many years in the minors], chances are he'll be spending another year in the minors. We are usually pretty accurate."

Berger is also knowledgeable about any trades that might be brewing. "I remember one player with the Chicago Cubs when he was a kid first coming up. He still has a couple of good years left in him.

Right now, he thinks he's going to be traded, and he may be right."

A team roster with certain penciled-in data is then brought over. "Now, take the Chicago White Sox, for instance," Berger says. "This is a pretty set team." He runs his finger down the list. "Take a guy like Hector Torres. He's been around a while, but we just don't think he'll make this ball club. So we didn't print his picture."

The fateful decision of whose picture will be printed rests solely on Berger's shoulders. "It's really tough. You can't imagine what it's like to go down to spring training, have a guy ask, 'Where's my card?' and have to tell him, 'Gee, I didn't print your picture this year.' "

Ballplayers tend to be more than casually interested in their cards. In pitcher Jim Bouton's best-selling book, *Ball Four*, he writes, "Someone once asked Al Ferrara of the Dogers why he wanted to be a baseball player. He said because he always wanted to see his picture on a bub-ble-gum card. Well, me too. It's an ego trip."

Berger finds this to be true. "It's like the actor or movie star who makes it to the top and gets his name in lights. When a player makes the majors and gets his picture on a baseball card, he feels he has made it. I have had many of them tell me it was their biggest thrill ever."

Players can also be touchy about their photos. "They will sometimes complain that they don't like their picture," says Berger. "It's usually because they don't like the angle or weren't shaved. As a result, there are a few players who insist on seeing the pictures to be used. They realize the importance of a good image to the kids and so they want to be shown at their very best. They hate being depicted looking unkempt. As a result, we specifically write to the players' representatives as to when photographers will be there. But there is only so much we can do. You can't make a silk purse out of a sow's ear!"

# 4
# A Museum Visit

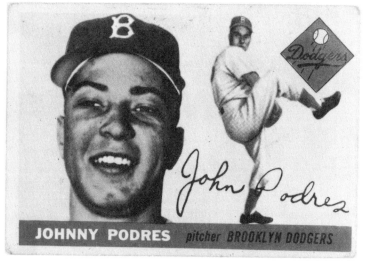

The Metropolitan Museum of Art in New York City is one of the world's greatest museums. Within its immense interior are some of the most precious art treasures ever assembled. Relics from the early Chinese dynasties, pottery from the Incas, African art, French impressionism, pop art, photography — the best of these, and more, are on display. People from all over the world put the Metropolitan Museum of Art on their itinerary whenever they visit New York City.

Yet all the prestige and availability of expensive paintings and sculptures has not diluted the popularity of the mammoth card collection of the late Jefferson Burdick, located in the museum's Print Study Department. It comprises some 660 bound albums that fill several ten-foot shelves.

Within each album are thousands of cards on a multitude of subjects. There are cards on countries, birds, flowers, flags, buildings, ships. On dolls, soldiers, statesmen, boxers, poets. On movie stars, airplanes, Indian chiefs, stamps. On circuses, nursery rhymes, guns, butterflies. On dancers, cities, states, games. And on baseball players.

According to museum employees, most visitors on almost any given day come solely to see the more than 200,000 baseball cards — the largest collection of such cards in the world. Appointments must be made in advance. Children are allowed in only when accompanied by a parent, and no one under ten is permitted entrance.

But exceptions can be made. "Recently," said a museum employee, "a woman brought her son, who was nine, here. She said he was a very serious collector. We let him in. She later said that if we would not have let him in, she would have lied about his age the next time they came.

"People come from faraway places. A family from California drove here just to see the collection and returned afterward without even staying in the city overnight. A woman from Peru was here a few months ago. She said her son, who was a collector, couldn't come, so he had sent her."

Indeed, in checking the guest book (which everyone must sign), addresses from all over the United States, Canada, and South America are in evidence. Under "reason for coming," most visitors write: "To see the baseball-card collection." Most of them are serious collectors themselves. A majority seem to be pre-teenagers.

With so many avid collectors around, there might be some concern about security. Fortunately, though, there doesn't seem to be. "Actually, it's just the opposite," said an employee. "While there has never been any card stealing, there have been many instances where someone will bring to our attention a card that is loose or damaged."

Museum employees, however, carefully observe visitors to make sure that there are no pens used around the collection. They also make sure that the pages and cards, some rather fragile from age, are handled tenderly.

What of the man who is solely responsible for this collection? Jefferson Burdick, a native of Syracuse, New York, worked on electronics parts in a factory there and authored *The American Card Catalogue*, which is the collector's checklist.

His baseball-card collection extends from the 1880's, when cards were included with Old Judge Cigarettes, to the 1955 Topps and Bowman Gum cards.

Hyatt Mayor, curator emeritus of the museum's Print and Photograph Department, remembers Jefferson Burdick well. "It was in the late 1950's that this man, bent over from arthritis, came to me from right off the street and asked if we would be interested in exhibiting his collection," Mayor recalls. "I said we would be. At the time, though, I had no idea of the size of the collection."

Mayor admired Burdick a great deal. "Burdick was a sedentary man because of his affliction," said Mayor, "yet he still managed to correspond with collectors all over the world. He developed the whole business of card collecting — swapping, cataloguing, and so forth. He had great courage."

It took Burdick over two years of continuous work to mount his prodigious collection. Though his fingers were gnarled by arthritis, he managed to finish the project in the winter of 1963. The following day he entered a hospital, where he eventually died.

The cards are classified according to product manufacturer, and are in separate albums. This is convenient and useful for examining the baseball cards. By perusing the tobacco albums, then the candy (caramel) albums, and finally the gum albums,

CHASE. N. Y. AMER.

"HANK" GREENBERG

"ARKY" VAUGHAN

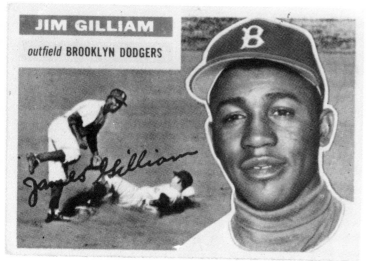

JIM GILLIAM

outfield BROOKLYN DODGERS

DON Drysdale

BROOKLYN DODGERS PITCHER

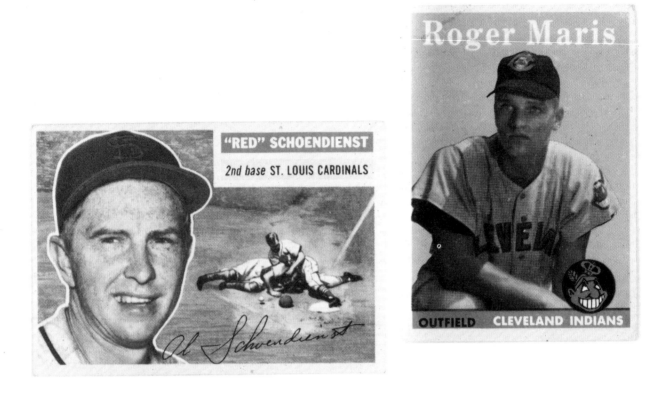

one gets to see the cards in their true chronological order. One can see their evolution from year to year.

And now for the cards themselves.

## Tobacco

The tobacco cards are primarily in albums 246 and 247. Most of them are much smaller than the modern card. Among the companies issuing such cards in the late 1880's and early 1900's were American Beauty, Lenox, Tolstoi, Polar Bear, Uzit, Hindu, Carolina Brights, El Principe, De Gales, Broad Leaf, Old Mill, Sweet Caporal, Piedmont, Sovereign, Old Judge, Cycle, Recruit, and Obak.

For the most part, the cards (1½″ by 2½″) are crude photos of the players, in color, all wearing well-starched uniforms.

Fatima Turkish Blend Cigarettes issued handsome team photos that were much larger than the standard tobacco card.

Hassan Cork Tip Cigarettes manufactured one of the more unusual cards of that (or any) time, a black-and-white action shot centered between two small headshots in color. On one card, for example, one may see pictures of Eddie Collins and Home Run Baker. In the center is an action shot of Baker playing third. On the back is a description of the action: "This photo shows the 1911 idol of the fans, Home Run Baker, making a putout from his vantage point at third. Baker was born

34

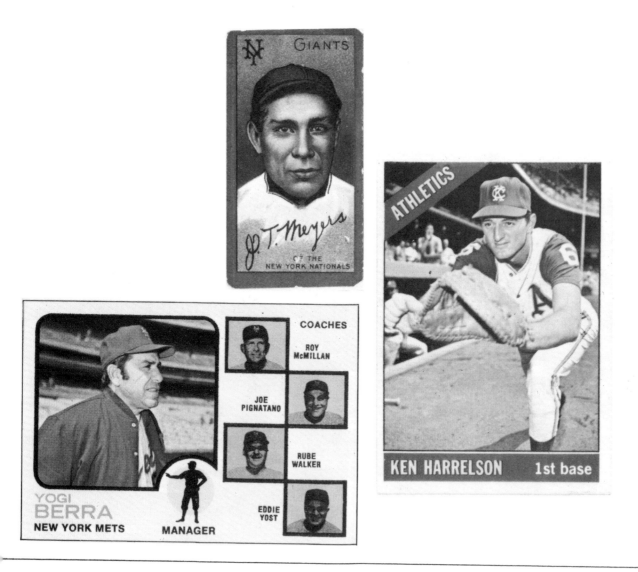

on a farm in Triappe, Md., in 1886, and he has remained a farmer ever since." The heading on the card reads: "Baker Gets His Man."

Mayo's had color cartoons based on baseball expressions. "Strike One" is the caption above a picture of a man getting hit with a policeman's billy. "Put Out at First" shows someone evicted from his apartment and whose furniture is out on First Street.

Another interesting series, the Baseball Folder cards, is made up of cards with foldover illustrations — one player is visible when the card is folded over. Presto! He is gone and another player takes his place when the card is opened up. Two separate biographies grace the back of the card, but, given the crude illustrations, unless one player is winding up (obviously a pitcher) and the other fielding a groundball, one is hard put to know which player is which.

Ramly Turkish Cigarettes issued handsome photos with gold borders, while Recruit had cards with a brown background. Old Mills had a red border around its small black-and-white photos.

Most, but not all of the cards, have biographies and some statistics on their backs. The anecdotes make interesting reading. One, for example, reads, "On his Day on August 12, 1908, Cy Young was presented with the entire receipts of the game and more silverware and floral designs than he could carry." An early card of Charles

Street reveals that Street was the first man ever to catch a ball dropped from the Washington Monument.

Tobacco cards also issued series cards with pictures of minor-league players. Red Sun Cigarettes included small green cards with players from the Southern Association who played for teams like Mobile, Nashville, and New Orleans. Obak Mouthpieces had players from the Pacific Coast and Northwestern Leagues, playing for teams like Victoria, Vancouver, Seattle, Tacoma, and Portland. Complimentary blurbs on the backs of the cards never indicated any worse characteristic than "steady," or "hard-working."

Sweet Caporal, in addition to their standard-sized card, manufactured domino disks, which had players on one side and dominos in various positions on the reverse side.

All of these cards came out in the early days of the business. The only tobacco company with cards in this album that were printed much later is Red Man. With each package of Red Man's Chewing Tobacco in 1953 and 1954 came color photos of players like Willie Mays, Richie Ashburn, Stan Musial, and Mickey Mantle, with short biographies and statistical information in a box to the left of the photo.

## Candy

The candy cards, principally in albums 316 and 317, disclose a wider assortment than the tobacco cards. Some of them are of quite high quality, while others are not. One set has color drawings of players in action — a pitcher winding up, a catcher gazing up into the sun for a supposed pop-up. In the background, sometimes red, sometimes threatening, skies are visible. Another set is composed of small head-shots — Frank Chance (of Evers-to-Tinker-to-Chance fame) is portrayed wearing a well-starched collar and with his hair parted in the middle.

Base Ball Caramels contained 33 cards in every set. Only players from three teams are shown in each individual set. The illustrations are all somewhat similar. Players seem to be either leaning on a bat (the

JIM MALONEY  pitcher

CARL HUBBELL

hitters) or throwing (pitchers). What is perhaps more remarkable, though, is that the faces of several of the players are exactly the same! On the New York Giants, an outfielder named John ("Red") Murray, who compiled a .270 batting average in 12 years in the majors, is an exact duplicate of pitcher Luther ("Dummy") Taylor, who once lost 27 games in one season for the Giants and was exiled to Cleveland before returning to New York. Both are shown catching a ball over their right shoulders. In a set of pitchers, Rube Marquard, a Hall of Famer who once won 73 games for the Giants in three years, happens to have the same face and windup as another star, hurler Joe ("Iron Man") McGinnity, who in seven years won between 22 and 35 games annually. Both played for the Giants in 1908, only that was Marquard's first year and McGinnity's last.

John H. Dockman & Son issued cards of 50 Prominent Members of the National and American Leagues. One was packaged with every piece of Base Ball Gum. These cards are very much like the Base Ball Caramels.

The cards from Croft's Swiss Milk Cocoa, "served hot at our fountain (South 15th Street, Philadelphia), Montagne & Co.," are a bit better, though they show some ludicrous poses. A picture of Hugh Jennings, Detroit Tiger manager in 1910-11, depicts him jumping up and down and cheering on the sidelines. That may have been what managers did in those days.

Standard Caramels had a much improved card with clearer pictures of the players in simple headshots. Similar are the Caramel Company of Philadelphia cards, except in this set the players appear to be wearing rouge on their cheeks and thick red lipstick.

The G. A. Bigge Company shows players from the Coast League. Players have names across their shirts like Vernon, San Francisco, Los Angeles, Sacramento, and Oakland. Most are in color.

Naja, Mello Mart, and Prominent Base Ball Players are all small black-and-white cards. American Caramel of Lancaster and York (Pennsylvania) has a set of 240 cards, all black-and-white, with a mirror-like border around them. The cards with a

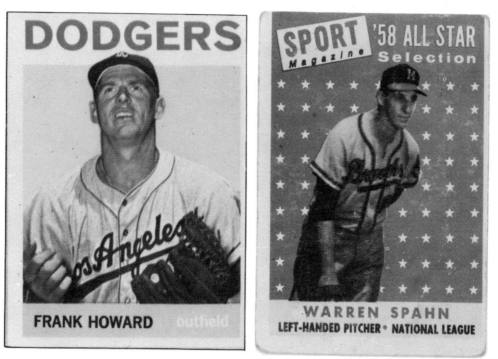

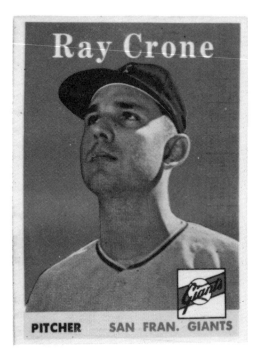

Ray Crone

PITCHER    SAN FRAN. GIANTS

BILL SKOWRON

first base NEW YORK YANKEES

Bill Skowron

KANSAS CITY    OUTFIELD

AMOS OTIS    ROYALS

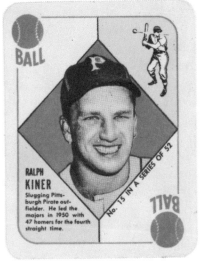

BALL

RALPH
KINER

Slugging Pitts-
burgh Pirate out-
fielder. He led the
majors in 1950 with
47 homers for the fourth
straight time.

No. 15 IN A SERIES OF 52

BALL

brown hue are American League players, the ones with a grayish tint are players in the National League.

Zeenut put out some very handsome cards. These are long brown cards showing posed action. Zeenut also did cards on minor leaguers.

Cracker Jack Players has a red background with players again wearing rouge and lipstick. Biographies are on the backs.

C&B Chewing Gum (some of the early gum cards are in the candy albums) has each player pictured in a colorful headshot. So professional are the photos that each player looks more like an early 20th century statesman.

Stars of the Diamond, which came in every five-cent package of Colgan's Violet Chips and Mint Chip ("Beware of imitations," reads the back), are small black-and-white pictures with player and team name on the card.

## Gum

Most of the early gum cards of the 1930's and early 1940's were put out by the Goudey Co. These cards, unlike most of the candy cards and more like the earlier tobacco cards, have a good deal of biographical data on the backs. "The Mad Russian of Baseball has put life in the Chicago Cubs. Novikoff hit a nice .300 in 1942 and played a spectacular game in the field," reads one. In another, "Hank Greenberg has been voted the most valuable player in baseball twice. In 1938, Hank hit 58 home runs, within two of the all-time record. Hank is in the army now, and doing a swell job there, too."

Goudey changed their card make-up often. Some of their cards are color illustrations, others are full-length black-and-white photos that include the player's autograph. Other Goudey cards have help-

ful hints on the backs — "Run out grounders, don't watch ball, watch coach. He should motion you whether to turn toward second or cross first base." Another card tells how to lay out a baseball diamond for boys 16 and under. It indicates that the pitcher's mound should be 50 feet away from home plate and the bases 82 feet apart.

The National Chicle Company issued cards in the 1920's and 1930's. In addition to their basic cards, which are well-done and in color, there are several comic cards. One shows Nick Altrock and Al Schacht as clowns — one is dressed as a cop holding a nightstick, the other is dressed as a bum trying to steal a base. Both are wearing baseball pants. Another shows Lloyd and Paul Waner being lifted by Pirate teammate Big Jim Warner.

The Big League Chewing Gum cards of 1933 are head shots in color. Each card has an anecdotal biography on the back: Floyd ("Babe") Herman — "Boy, can he hit the ball! . . . Broke in with a wallop." George Pipgras — "Used to be wild as a hawk." Frank Hogan — "He's a hard hitter when he lands on the ball."

The 1934 card of Big League has a diamond around the cards. On the bottom of each card is a "Lou Gehrig says," or "Chuck Klein says." Nice things are then said about their fellow players on the back.

On Lou Gehrig's own card, it said: "I would like every boy to be a member of the Knot Hole League of America because this league can help you to become a better ballplayer. It also makes it possible for boys to get base balls, gloves and uniforms without cost and I know that boys who have these things have more interest in the game and therefore, become better ballplayers. I will gladly write and answer any questions about the game that a member of the Knot Hole League of America

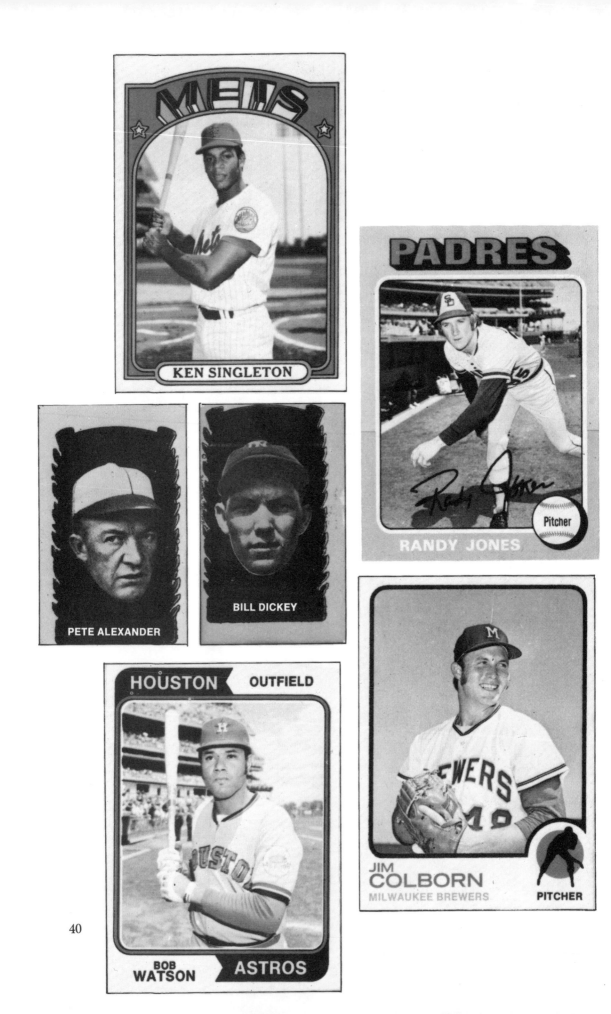

METS

KEN SINGLETON

PADRES

RANDY JONES

Pitcher

PETE ALEXANDER

BILL DICKEY

HOUSTON OUTFIELD

BOB WATSON ASTROS

JIM COLBORN
MILWAUKEE BREWERS PITCHER

writes me about baseball. Send your letters to me care of Knot Hole League of America, 52 Everett Street, Allston, Mass."

The 1936 cards have a game on the back. For example, a card might say, "FOUL BALL — Over the catcher's head and into the screen," or "HOME RUN — A terrific drive into left field bleachers. It's over 400 feet out there."

Big League's 1938 cards have an illustration of the player's body drawn to an oversized face. Small cartoons are on the front of the card as well. For example, on Joe DiMaggio's card is a picture of a ballplayer carrying a bag with $25,000 written on it. Underneath is the caption, "Pretty fair salary for a young fellow."

The 1941 Big League cards show each player in the same pose in four different colors — red, green, yellow and blue.

National Chicle had cards that provided playing tips. Pitching Tips are given by Lefty Grove. For instruction on the fastball, Lefty says, "Boys under sixteen should be careful not to overwork or strain their arms in trying for too much speed." Infielder Rabbit Maranville of the old Boston Braves did a tip series on how to slide, run bases, hit, and pitch. (How would he know?)

Schuitter-Johnson had a card, all in red, on how to throw the curve, fade away, etc., including illustrations.

In 1948, Leaf Gum provided cards with small head shots of the players. Bowman, in that year, had a black-and-white posed picture of each player. The following year they went to a color backdrop with colored uniforms. The uniform color is obviously drawn in. In 1953, however, the Bowman color is authentic. In their 1955 series, each player is shown within a TV screen.

The earliest cards from Topps are in the 1951 Foul Ball Series. The player's face is within a diamond, and his name is outside..

A trip to the Metropolitan Museum of Art seems a must for anyone really interested in baseball cards. Perusal of the Burdick albums will in itself give one a good look at baseball-card history. It will give the baseball-card neophyte an opportunity to see what cards once looked like and how they have changed. The collector will be able to see exactly what he might want to buy or trade for. And the collector-to-be can decide upon the cards with which he would like to begin his collection.

Of course, the Museum's original cards are not for sale, but prints of them may be purchased.

# 5
# Goofs

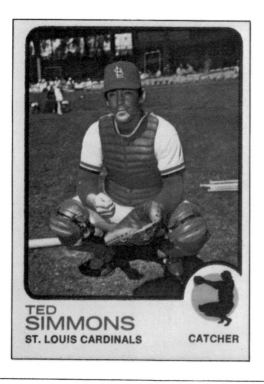

TED
SIMMONS
ST. LOUIS CARDINALS                    CATCHER

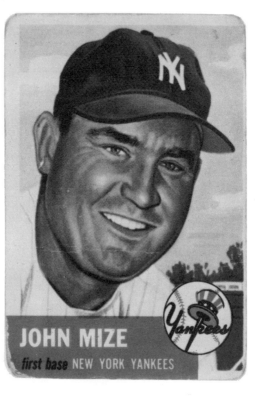

JOHN MIZE
*first base* NEW YORK YANKEES

Did you know that in the history of the baseball card, its various manufacturers have managed to picture: a) a person who never played any kind of professional baseball; b) several ballplayers hitting and throwing in a manner they never did professionally; c) players from a team that never existed; and d) a player who never wanted his picture taken?

All of the above has happened, which is not to say necessarily that the producers of baseball cards have been bunglers. It's just that, as in any large operation, un-usual and sometimes embarrassing mistakes will be made. If General Motors or Ford has the right to produce a lemon of a car every now and then, then surely Topps Chewing Gum and its baseball-card-producing predecessors have a similar right.

Topps' Sy Berger is ready to admit that human and technological error has played a part in the making of certain baseball cards over the past two and a half decades of Topps reign. He is not especially pleased about it, either.

"In this business," Berger relates, "we have a tremendous responsibility to the kids. The baseball card is the gospel, the Talmud. They have nothing else to go on. If we make a mistake, it would be like giving a kid an erroneous primer to read."

And who picks up most of the errors? "Youngsters are tremendously observant. Every error we make, the kids pick it up immediately, yet we make far fewer errors than any sports book I've ever seen."

The first big baseball-card boner came long before either Berger or Topps arrived on the scene. It goes back to the days when the airplane and the automobile were still in their infancy.

Yet, in some circles he's best remembered today because he didn't smoke cigarettes.

Tobacco companies were the first to produce baseball cards, but since Wagner didn't smoke, he didn't want to promote the habit among the youth of his day, so he forbade the manufacturer of Sweet Caporal Cigarettes from distributing his card. His card had already been printed, however, and a few of them had gone out. These half dozen or so cards that circulated are considered a rare prize by collectors today and worth considerable money on the open market.

Another tobacco card, this one of a Philadelphia outfielder named Magee, is in

In 1908 there was an infielder for the Pittsburgh Pirates named Honus Wagner who would be rated as one of the greatest ballplayers in history. Wagner played for 21 years and had an all-time batting average of .328. He could hit and run and field.

error — the player's name is misspelled Magie.

Topps has made some interesting goofs in its time. Most embarrassing, perhaps, is the case of the "non-ballplayer." With the look of a man who has just stepped on a thorn, Berger recalls the incident: "In 1969, our photographer went down to spring training camp to shoot pictures. . . . He mistook a young Spanish boy in an Angels' uniform to be [third baseman] Aurelio Rodriguez. As a result, we printed a picture that year of the Angel batboy."

And so goes the story of how a smiling batboy wormed his way into baseball-card immortality.

"In our 1972 ERA Leaders card," Berger recalls, "instead of a picture of Dave Roberts of San Diego, who had finished second to Tom Seaver in that category, we had a picture of another San Diego pitcher, Danny Coombs.

cards had been distributed. Now it's a rare card worth about $5."

Topps' most notorious error, according to Berger, and the one most often written about, occurred in 1959. This was during the short period of domination the Milwaukee Braves enjoyed in the National League. The Braves had just run away from the Dodgers and the Giants during 1958 to take the pennant before going on to trounce the Yankees in the World Series. The aces of the Milwaukee staff were a stylish left-hander named Warren Spahn and a hard-throwing righty named Lew Burdette. Spahn had won 21 games that year, and Burdette 20, plus three in the

"In 1952, we had the pictures of Yankees' Joe Page and Johnny Sain transposed. The faces that had been pasted on the frame fell off and were put back incorrectly. A printer caught the error, but not until the plates had been made and several

World Series. As it turned out, they were also quite successful in the practical joke department.

While a Topps photographer was shooting the Brave players during spring training, the two pitchers decided to have

Victor Raschi

AURELIO
RODRIGUEZ
3rd Base

ANGELS

ORIOLES

Harry D Brecheen

HARRY BRECHEEN coach BALTIMORE ORIOLES

ATHLETICS

COLLINS PHILA. AMER.

Burdette pose with the glove on his right hand, giving the appearance of a left-hander.

"We didn't catch it," Berger sighs. "As soon as the card hit the market, we started getting calls and letters. 'YOU MADE A MISTAKE! YOU MADE A MISTAKE!' The kids are pretty sharp."

In addition, the 1959 Lew Burdette card also had his first name misspelled L-O-U. But that was something Burdette and Spahn had never planned.

Several years later, a veteran utility infielder with the Pirates named Gene Freese was photographed as a left-handed hitter. Freese never performed from the left side of the plate in his stint in the majors. He was so successful at his gag, however, that he posed as a lefty swinger the following year as well.

"Every young player tries to pull that gag now," said Berger, "so we give each of our photographers a roster that briefs them on how each player bats and throws."

Another player portrayed in an unnatural (for him) batting stance was Henry ("Hank") Aaron on his 1957 card. Hammerin' Hank was not really trying to pull a fast one, either. A technical problem caused the negative to be reversed, and it wound up showing Aaron batting left-handed. The giveaway is the No. 44 on Hank's jersey. In the photo, it is reversed. Aaron never hit one of his career-record major-league blasts lefty.

The faces of some players have been inadvertently switched at times. In 1952, Topps' card No. 391 is supposedly that of Ben Chapman. Instead, while Ben's name and performance statistics are on the card, the face is that of Sam Chapman. Both were outfielders who played during the same time.

In the following year, card No. 219

of then Senator infielder Pete Runnels has a picture of Washington teammate Don Johnson. Six years later, in 1959, the baseball card of Ralph Lumenti (No. 316) is mistakenly graced with the face of Camilo Pascual. A year before, Giants' Mike McCormick (No. 37) had his own card, but the wrong face, that of teammate Ray Monzant.

Chicago White Soxers J. C. Martin and Gary Peters are transposed on their cards of 1960. Peters' card (No. 407) shows Martin, and Martin's card (No. 346) shows Peters.

In 1963, Topps juggled the faces of two bespectacled wild ex-Yankee pitchers, Eli Grba and Ryne Duren. On card No. 231, Grba's name inaccurately identifies the likeness of the even wilder and more near-sighted Duren.

In 1965, the card is that of a bonus baby, yet major-league flop, named Lew Krausse (No. 462), but the face is that of a "who's he?" named Pete Lovrich.

Topps made a rather embarrassing error in the series of 1966. Chicago Cub pitcher Dick Ellsworth was the man the company meant to display on card No. 447. Instead, a photograph of Ken Hubbs appeared. The company had been preparing a memorial card that year for Hubbs, killed two years before in an airplane tragedy.

In Topps' Tigers' Rookies of 1967 (No. 72), the name of George Korince identifies the photo of James Brown. In Brewers' Rookies of 1972 (No. 162), the identifications of Jerry Bell and Darrell Porter are transposed. In both cases, only their mothers really knew.

In 1973, the World Champion Oakland Athletics had two of their stars misrepresented. On Joe Rudi's card (No. 360), the Oakland outfielder bears a striking resemblance to teammate Gene Tenace.

In 1975, Kansas City Royal catcher Fran

Healy's face appears on batterymate Steve Busby's card, and catcher Dave Duncan appears on Larry Haney's card.

Back in 1961, many but not all of the cards featuring Mudcat Grant erroneously identified him as Brooks Lawrence.

Additional errors have home-run king Roger Maris, then with the St. Louis Cardinals, depicted in his old New York Yankee uniform. In 1974, the name of New York Met relief pitcher Bob Apodaca is spelled Apadaca.

a gamble that fell flat on its face. Rumors were circulating at the time that the financially troubled San Diego Padres would pick up their franchise and move east to the nation's capital. With this in mind, some of the Padre players had their cards released with "Washington" as the team name. But when the team was saved for San Diego by a man who deals in hamburgers on a large scale, Topps was left with a bit of egg on its face.

Today, most of the goof cards are worth

Other cards have been printed with wrong backs or incorrect statistics. The 1964 Rookie Card of Phillie Dave Bennett reads: "The 19-year-old right-handed curveballer is just 18 years old." A pretty good trick.

Perhaps the latest boner of any consequence would be Topps' gamble of 1974,

a premium on the swapping market. The extra money each mistake will bring is dependent upon the number of cards released before the error was corrected. In most cases, an entire set may have been distributed before the mistake was detected, causing no significant reevaluation. With say, the old Honus Wagner card,

48

however, where very few circulated, upward of $1,000 has been demanded and received. A goof card which has gone through a full printing may only be worth from one to five dollars.

In any case, while the baseball-card people may not be thrilled over having their goofs exploited, finding a mistake here and there simply adds credence to the maxim that "nobody is perfect."

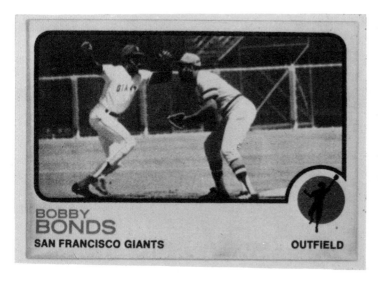

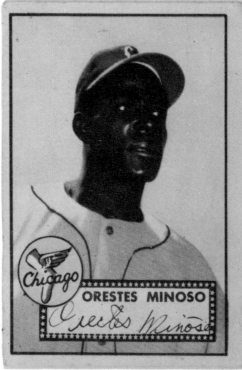

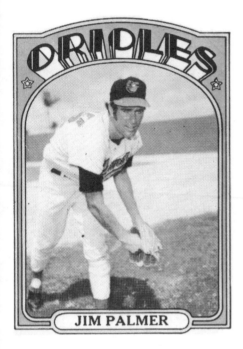

JIM PALMER

jim bunning

DETROIT TIGERS
PITCHER

VERN LAW
pitcher PITTSBURGH PIRATES

# 6
# The Collectors

Depending on whom you talk to, there are somewhere between 10,000 and 500,000 serious baseball card collectors in America. In the last few years, as everyone associated with collecting will tell you, the growth of the hobby has been enormous.

But who is the card collector, what cards does he look for, how long has he collected, and why?

The collector may be a doctor, an accountant, a sportswriter, a businessman, or a college student. He may have begun collecting several years ago or half a century ago. He may search solely for certain cards or he may be trying to complete entire sets.

And he collects — well, for a thousand different reasons.

One of the largest collections extant is maintained by Irving Lerner, an accountant from Philadelphia. Lerner estimates that he has over 100,000 baseball cards in his collection. He is a frequent visitor to card conventions.

"I grew up in a poor neighborhood," Lerner recalls. "As kids, we used baseball cards like money. If someone had something you wanted, you'd offer him baseball cards for it. I was lucky because my father owned a candy store, and while I never had much money to spend, I always had

51

plenty of baseball cards in my pockets."

Lerner publishes *Who's Who in Card Collecting,* a listing of the country's most prominent card collectors. He has also established the Card Collectors Hall of Fame. The first man chosen for it was Jefferson Burdick of Syracuse.

As Lerner puts it, "I collect all sorts of cards — from tobacco to food to gum. People are always writing me, wanting to make trades, and so forth. I sell my duplicates, so I can turn over my money and buy more cards."

Lerner has the rare Honus Wagner card, worth up to $1,500, but cherishes some of his other cards more. "My favorite cards are the Lumis Peanut Butter cards that were put out during the early 1950's. Few collectors have these cards."

And why does he collect? "There is nostalgic value in it. It is a good way to remember one's childhood heroes. Plus, it is a good way to relax."

Another advanced collector is Wayne Varner, a stockbroker from Pittsburgh. Varner started collecting as a youngster, but gave it up when he got married. Only in the past few years has Varner picked up the hobby again. He's made up for lost time, though, having attended 13 conventions across the country in a 14-month span.

"I buy mostly from people who don't want their cards any more. I also check ads in local newspapers," Varner discloses.

Among the cards he traded for are regional cards from the 1950's, like cards from Dandy Potato Chips issued in Pittsburgh, Lumis Peanut Butter in Philadelphia, Kahn's Wieners in Pittsburgh and Cleveland, and Drake's Cookies throughout most of the East. "I'll also trade for West Coast regional cards like Bell Brand Potato Chips," says Varner.

Varner has his prejudicies. "I'm not too hot on tobacco cards, for a number of rea-

sons. First of all, tobacco cards are not worth as much as other cards. You had to pay for other cards, but tobacco cards were given away free with the product. Also, the tobacco cards aren't terribly attractive. The full name of the player does not appear on the card, and more than one card was put out, because a single series ran for several years. Additionally, the cards aren't numbered, so it makes it difficult to collect [card collectors trade and deal by number, not name]. Finally, there are usually no bios on the backs of the cards."

Varner lists two cards picturing superstars among the personal favorites in his collection. These are the 1952 Topps' Mickey Mantle and the 1954 Ted Williams issued by Bowman. In 1954, the Bowman people had mistakenly issued two cards with the identical number, No. 66. The other No. 66 was Williams' zany Boston Red Sox teammate, Jimmy Piersall. In the checklist that year, Williams was somehow omitted. The error, plus Williams' superstar status, make this card especially valuable.

Another card Varner treasures, though worth less on the market, is a 1954 Dandy Potato Chip card of Paul Smith. Smith was a Pirate outfielder who spent four undistinguished seasons in the majors. But the limited quantity of Smith's card, rather than his baseball achievements, makes this a coveted card.

Varner gives some good pointers to youngsters trying to get into the card-collecting hobby. "The condition of the card is very important. A card in mint condition is worth twice as much as a card that is in poor condition. Keep your cards in good shape. Subscribe to hobby publications, so you can trade with others. Be aware of values, understand supply and demand. For more experienced traders, a clearing house is a good place to pick up cards."

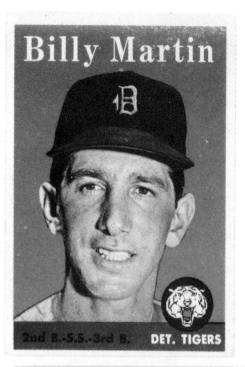

Billy Martin

2nd B.-S.S.-3rd B.    DET. TIGERS

PITCHER
TIGERS

MICKEY
LOLICH

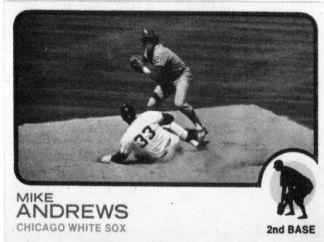

MIKE
ANDREWS
CHICAGO WHITE SOX

2nd BASE

TOPPS
ALL-STAR
ROOKIE

JIM RICE

OUTFIELD
RED SOX

53

A clearing house, also called an auction, is run periodically by people who advertise the selling of their cards, usually through the classified ads in local newspapers.

Another notable collector was Tommy Holmes, a former sportswriter for the *Brooklyn Eagle* and the *New York Herald-Tribune*. Brought up on a farm in a small village in Suffolk County, New York, Holmes began collecting all types of sporting cards as a youngster. He received his first card on July 4, 1910 — it pictured two boxers, Jack Johnson and Jim Jeffries. Shortly afterward, he began collecting baseball cards. "I would mooch off friends," he said, "since only tobacco companies put out cards and no one in my family smoked."

Holmes stored his collection at his home in the Flatbush section of Brooklyn, not far from where the Dodgers once played. The cards were kept neatly bound in large loose-leaf albums. Holmes knew the background of his cards, and much about the men pictured on them.

"These cards," Holmes would point out, "are from the period 1907-1910 and are made from German dyes. World War I cut off the supplies and later the process became too expensive . . . The cards are all of minor-league players. I bought them for $25. They are worth $80 now."

Holmes was equally familiar with the derivations of the teams of yesterday, like the Brooklyn Superbas and the Boston Rustlers. "The Brooklyn team was named after Hanlon's Superbas [Hanlon was the team owner], an acrobatic group that toured the music halls of the day. The Boston Rustlers were owned by a man named Russell, who sold them to a political leader named Gaffney, who renamed them the Braves."

The small faces on the tobacco cards seemed to come alive as Holmes recounted

their history . . . "Jack Warhop was a Yankee pitcher they called Chief. In reality, he was a Richmond [Virginia] Russian who dealt Babe Rube his first major-league home run . . . Owen Wilson of Pittsburgh holds the major-league record for triples for a season with 37, something no one knows or can understand. There were much better players on that same team . . . John 'Biscuit Pants' Tidings of the Philadelphia Nationals was the last player to wear a mustache until recent times . . . John 'Chief' Meyer was a Mission Indian from California who never played baseball until he attended Dartmouth College,

DENNY McLAIN PITCHER TIGERS

which was then a school for Indians . . . Mordecai 'Three-Fingers' Brown lost part of his fingers in a mine accident. . . ."

Holmes also told an interesting story about the prized Honus Wagner card. It seems that a friend of his, Willie Ratner, who owned one of these rare cards, received repeated inquiries and offers to buy the card from a Tennessee newspaperman named Wirt Gammon. Finally, Gammon mailed Ratner a blank check to fill in. Ratner wrote in only the original sum offered by the Tennessean — a mere pittance compared to later offers. Ratner had not been holding back, he told the buyer — he had simply wanted to keep the card. In effect, he gave the card away.

As for Holmes, himself, his reason for collecting was a rather simple one. "I collect old cards because I know there will never be any more of these."

lecting when I was 11, in 1951. This was during the infancy of modern card-collecting, which had not started again until 1948, after World War II. Since then, I've picked up cards every year."

Aronstein favors the Bowman, Topps and Fleers cards. Yet his card collection goes back to the earliest tobacco cards. Among the cards he owns are the two rarest and most sought-after of the tobacco cards, Honus Wagner and Eddie Plank, and one of the more significant gum cards, that of Napolean Lajoie. Eddie Plank was a pitcher of long standing for the Philadelphia Athletics, beginning at the turn of

Mike Aronstein is a former salesman from Yorktown, New York, who gave up his job to turn his sports-nostalgia hobby into a business venture. Aronstein estimates the number in his baseball-card collection at about 60,000. "I started collecting when I was 11, in 1951. This was the century. His card is rare, according to Aronstein, because the plate was accidentally destroyed after only a few cards had been printed. Lajoie (a Hall of Fame player and manager) was No. 106 in the 1934 Goudey series. "Somehow, his card was messed up in 1933," relates Aronstein, "so the card was reissued in 1934 with its 1933 format. But that series only went up to No. 96, so the only way to get the card was by writing in to the company."

Aronstein sells old baseball cards and other sports memorabilia at his stores in Cooperstown, New York (site of the baseball Hall of Fame), and Upper Saddle River, New Jersey. At his stores and at conventions he sells such items as *Sports Americana*, a complete baseball-card checklist from 1948 to the present; old strip cards from the 1920's; albums for mounting or displaying baseball cards; and his own set of baseball cards of league leaders, great teams, minor-league players, and present-day Yankees and Mets.

Through the mail, from ads in *Sporting News*, or from stores or conventions, one can acquire color pictures of teams such as the Cedar Rapids Giants, the Iowa Oaks, the Waterloo Dodgers; and such unknown players as Karel DeLeeuw, Bobby Edmondson, and other minor-leaguers.

Unlike many baseball-card collectors, Woody Gelman is not an avid fan of the sport, or terribly knowledgeable about it. This was to his advantage recently when he appeared on the TV show, "To Tell The Truth." The celebrity panel kept asking Gelman and the two impostors sports questions in order to find the "real" baseball-card collector. "Kitty Carlisle, who knows less baseball than I do," said Gelman, "asked me how Babe Ruth got his name. I told her that when he hit the ball, the ball was hit with such force it went 'bam.' From bam came bambino, which can be translated to Babe." In any case, the panel was stumped — no one picked Woody Gelman as the real Woody Gelman.

Gelman began collecting as a kid in 1922. "I had a fondness for strip cards [ten cards to a strip]. Two strips would cost a penny. Today they go for $3 per card."

Gelman also differs from other baseball-card collectors in that he collects all forms of pop art. "The growth of pop art," Gelman says, "is simultaneous with the growth of the nation. The first cards issued were those of generals, Civil War scenes, scenes of Central Park. As a boy, I collected all of these."

After putting aside his baseball cards for many years, Gelman happened to walk into a neighborhood candy store in 1945, where he saw strip cards. "No one had been buying the cards, so when I asked the store owner how much, his wife said, 'Why don't you just give them to him?' which he did. Not too long afterwards, I heard about Jeff Burdick. I became associated with him in the production of the *American Card Catalog* and took it over when he died. I'm currently revising it."

The *American Card Catalog* is now published under the aegis of Nostalgia Press, Gelman's own publishing firm. As with other books that Gelman publishes (and often illustrates and writes), the *American Card Catalog* is an extension of the publisher's collections.

"I tend to collect types of cards," says Gelman. "I try to have at least one card of every type mentioned in the card catalog.

"The value of cards has increased phenomenally. It has become the fastest-growing hobby in the United States, growing faster than stamps or coins.

"There are several reasons for collecting cards. Some people collect them as an investment, hoping for a capital gain. Many youths collect them because they are interested in baseball and want to be able to turn to a player's picture or statistic. Some collect them as a form of art expression, without any monetary motives. And some do it because it is a cheap way to keep up-to-date on sports."

Gelman may be termed a historian. In addition to cards, he collects everything

bill mazeroski

PITTSBURGH PIRATES
SECOND BASE

BOYHOOD PHOTOS
OF THE STARS

BUD HARRELSON

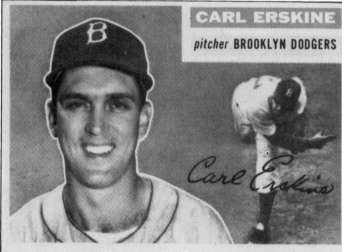

CARL ERSKINE

pitcher BROOKLYN DODGERS

Carl Erskine

N.Y.

MERKLE, N. Y. NAT'L

from comic books to old newspapers to girlie magazines — all with an eye toward the historical perspective.

Gelman follows this thinking in his baseball-card collection. "I am interested, say, in regional cards, but only to have them in historical context. By saying I collect types, I mean I save several examples to see what everything looked like, not being concerned with bulk or the time-consuming goal of completeness. I've sold cards of real value."

Gelman worked with Burdick in cataloguing the collection of cards exhibited at the Metropolitan Museum of Art, as well as the *American Card Catalog*. "Burdick was not monetarily oriented," said Gelman. "He would evaluate something as being worth a cent if he had never seen the card. I automatically figure such a card as worth fifty bucks."

Another old-time collector is Charles Bray of East Bangor, Pennsylvania. Bray was a co-author of the *American Card Catalog*, along with Burdick and Gelman. Bray, now in his 70's, first met Burdick in the mid-1930's. A former insurance man, Bray had collected baseball cards since early childhood. "Burdick and I both advertised for cards and we got to know each other," Bray recalled. "As I discovered new sets of cards, I would get in touch with him." And so began an imposing checklist.

Bray recently sold his entire card collection for an undisclosed sum to a noted collector in England named Worton-Tiger.

The East Bangor native has remained in the collecting hobby by publishing the *Card Collector's Bulletin*, "which gives me the function of a clearing house. I hold mail auctions four times a year."

As mentioned earlier, collectors can always be found wheeling and dealing at the many baseball-card conventions held throughout the country. At the 1975 convention in New York City's Greenwich Village, collectors of varying rank could be found peddling their wares, while keeping an eye out for any interesting cards to add to their own collections.

Two collectors, Ronnie Prager and Louis Michitsch, both of New York City, look for different cards for different reasons.

"I've been collecting since I was eight years old, back in 1948," says Prager. "I love baseball players. Through the cards, you remember what they look like, what their batting averages were.

"I like the gum cards of the 1950's. The art work is just not the same today. They really put quality into those old cards. The color was much richer." Prager pulls out a 1950's card of Billy Herman and a 1970 card of Steve Hargan to prove his point.

"The players looked much friendlier then. Look at this card of Phil Rizzuto. See the smile on his face? Now, that's a man! None of the cards today show that.

"My favorite card is one of Sid Gordon [an old infielder with the Giants, Red Sox and others in the 1940's and 1950's]. Gordon went to my junior high school.

RALPH BRANCA

BOB CLEMENTE
Outfield
Pittsburgh Pirates

DODGERS

SANDY KOUFAX pitcher

"As a kid I flipped and matched and traded. I have great memories of collecting cards of players and playing ball as a kid. If they hit a home run, you did.

"I look primarily for the pre-1955 cards at conventions. I sell my duplicates. If I find something else interesting, I'll put it in my collection. I picked up a 1954 Aaron here."

Louis Michitsch has been collecting for many years. "I'm crazy about all cards — tobacco, gum, Pacific Coast League, regional. I get my cards through trading and at shows like this one.

"I deal my duplicates so I can finance buying new cards. I have the 1933 Ruth and Gehrig put out by Goudey. I also have 36 cards in the 1949 Bowman set, which is worth about $2,000.

"I look to complete sets, and when I think about the cards I had in my hand as a kid, it kills me."

Collectors can be found just about anywhere throughout the United States, in big city and small town. One of the most extensive collectors is Larry Fritsch of Stevens Point, Wisconsin. Fritsch is co-compositor of the *Baseball Card Alphabetical Handbook,* which is a complete checklist of all Bowman, Fleers, Leaf, Topps, and Red Man cards from 1948 to the present.

Renata Galasso, a college student from the Bronx, New York, collects and sells baseball cards to finance her education. Dr. Joe Michalowicz, of Falls Church, Virginia, who specializes in later-issue cards, includes in his collection a poster of his all-time Washington Senators Turkey team,

highlighted by catcher Clyde Kluttz.

Frank Nagy, from Grosse Ile, Michigan, is an airport-tower official who is a household name in baseball-card collecting. His wife, Louise, relates a story to a reporter about how his hobby almost wrecked their marriage. "When we were first married, Frank drove to Pennsylvania to a card auction. He came home with over 400,000 cards that he had paid $4,000 for — our entire savings. One problem was that the weight of the cards caused the springs of our car to collapse. My dad said I should leave him."

Bob Rathgeber of Cincinnati, a longtime collector, recently made baseball-card history when he found "the most valuable baseball card in existence" — a 1910 card of Honus Wagner in a batting stance.

"All the other Wagner cards were the same portrait. Ours shows him batting — a card nobody even knew existed."

Rathgeber admits lucking into the card. Along with co-owners Dick Reuss and Tom Wickman, he bought a set of 300 old cards for about 40 cents a card from an antique dealer in Virginia. "We had no idea it was there. Our first reaction was, 'No, it can't be!' because no one had ever heard of such a card. So we took the card to a paper restoration expert and he authenticated it."

But of all the baseball-card collectors, the one who claims the greatest inventory of cards might very well be Bruce York of Georgetown, Connecticut. According to the authors of *The Great American Baseball Card,* York's warehouse contains a total of 10,000,000 cards.

# 7
# The Art of Collecting

MARQUARD, N. Y. Nat'l

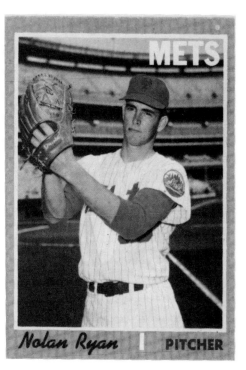

_Nolan Ryan_  PITCHER

MICKEY MANTLE
Outfield

New York
Yankees

It is early Sunday morning of an Indian summer day. The streets of New York City are quiet. Yet, at an old armory on Astor Place, on the fringe of Greenwich Village, people of various ages have already managed to rub sleep from their eyes. At the building's top floor they pay the necessary admission charge and enter the latest sports collectors convention.

Inside the convention room, men and women sit behind cafeteria-like tables. In front of them lies their merchandise.

There are buttons with inscriptions that read, "Go, Maury, Go," "Say Hey," and "Amazing Mets." There are cardboard stand-up figures of Hank and Willie and Ted and Joe. There are illustrations of Babe Ruth and Lou Gehrig in their prime. There are old magazines with faces of yesterday. And there are baseball cards, tons of baseball cards — tobacco cards, food cards, gum cards, candy cards, 3-D cards. Cards of recent Yankee players and cards of old Pacific Coast League stars. Cards with pictures nearly faded and cards with pictures that appear as if they were just taken. Cards in shoe boxes, albums, in rubber-banded stacks. On some there is the smell of gum, on others, the odor of mildew.

Sunday is the final day of the three-day convention. During this time an estimated 2,000 collectors have paid their admission to see what fellow collectors have to offer. Like horse buyers at a breeding auction, the players not only buy, but talk of past transactions and past winners. They talk shop.

Behind one table, two partners divide their bounty into Hall of Famers and non-Hall of Famers. "Is Sandy Koufax in the Hall of Fame? Well, then, he costs $1 more."

Youngsters are mesmerized by some of the more ancient cards. One of them ventures to ask a portly dealer (as if asking, "How much is that doggie in the window?"), "How much is that Joe DiMaggio?" Without pausing to look up from his collection, the man answers: "That's a 1939 DiMaggio worth $15 . . . if it was in perfect condition, it would be worth $25." The boy walks away, wishing he had never asked.

A young man, who apparently "knows his stuff" about collecting, makes the acquaintance of an old-time card master. They huddle. Perhaps some auspicious trade is in the offing.

A paunchy man who says he is in town to promote a rodeo inquires about the reasons for certain variation cards. A teenager wants to know how much he can get for a card with a Tom Seaver front and a Rico Petrocelli back.

The convention's organizer is Bob Gallagher. Gallagher takes time out from his job at Manufacturers Hanover Trust Company to run two conventions a year in New York. He charges $25 for a table, which is in effect a license to do business. A collector in his own right, he has been dealing in the cards for a few years. "The kids who come in here are usually hepped up on the superstars — Mays, Mantle, Aaron, DiMaggio, Williams, Musial. The older collectors come here to complete sets."

On Gallagher's own table is a large assortment of cards — Topps Double Header cards, old Goudey and Leaf cards, rare *Journal-American* cards. "The price of cards fluctuates according to supply and demand. This 1954 Aaron was worth $2 a few years ago. Today it goes for $12."

There are conventions today in many parts of the country. The bigger ones are held annually in Detroit (the biggest), Cincinnati, Philadelphia, New York, Los Angeles and Cambridge, Maryland. Yet, because nearby conventions are infrequent and travel is expensive, there are more practical ways to buy and sell cards.

One relatively inexpensive way is to place advertisements in local newspapers. Many collectors advertise under the "Wanted" or "Personal" sections of the classifieds. Weekly newspapers, or "Pennysavers," are considered especially good outlets for buying, selling, or trading baseball cards.

A phenomenon growing hand-in-hand with the popularity of card collecting is the increase of hobby publications. More regularly printed newspapers and magazines geared solely for collectors of sports nostalgia are available than ever before.

Experts in the field, all present or past collectors themselves, have found a market in publishing books on the hobby. Beginning with the original *American Card Catalog*, there are now at least a half dozen publications distributed through ads or at conventions.

The mail auction has drawn advanced

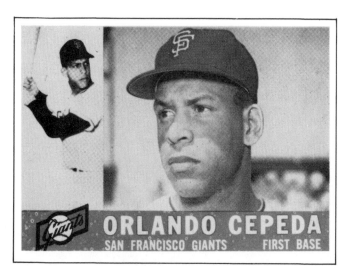

ORLANDO CEPEDA
SAN FRANCISCO GIANTS        FIRST BASE

JUAN MARICHAL        pitcher

lou burdette

MILWAUKEE BRAVES
PITCHER

BRAVES' FENCE BUSTERS
DEL CRANDALL · ED MATHEWS · HANK AARON · JOE ADCOCK

collectors to the fore in recent times. More people are auctioning their collection today, too, as the value of cards has sky-rocketed.

## Hobby Publications

*The Trader Speaks* is probably the most successful and accomplished of baseball-card periodicals. Owned and edited by Dan Dischley, the newspaper is published monthly at Lake Ronkonkoma, New York. It is heavy with advertising. $40 buys a full page ad (7½″ x 9″). A yearly subscription to the paper costs $9. There are approximately 10,000 subscribers.

Many collectors consider this the premier publication in the field. Besides the allotted space given to ads for buying and

SATCHELL PAIGE
pitcher ST. LOUIS BROWNS

ALVIN DARK
shortstop NEW YORK GIANTS

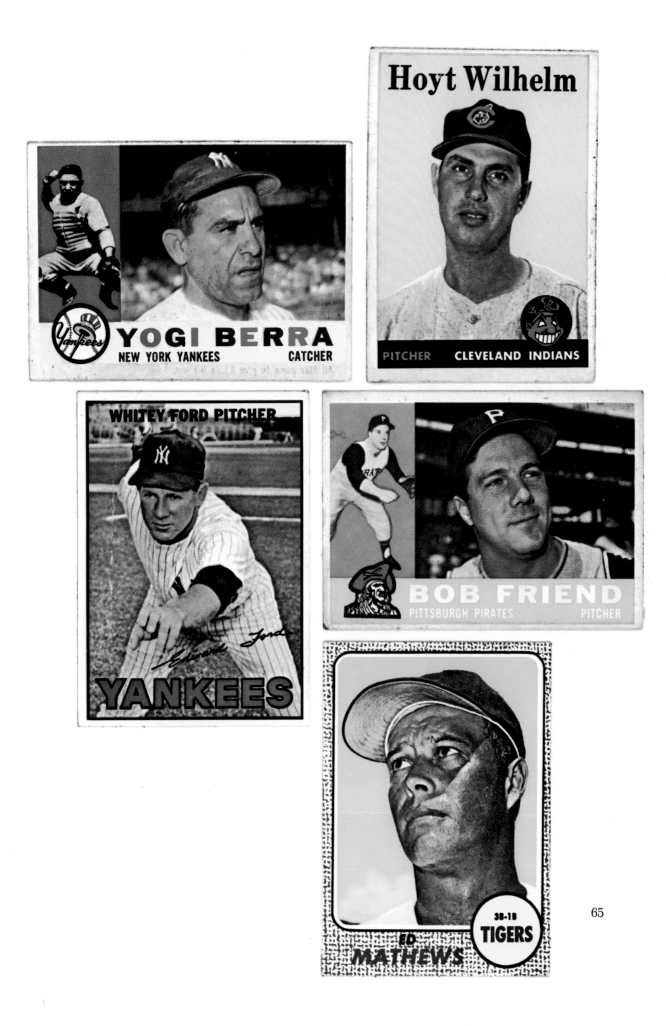

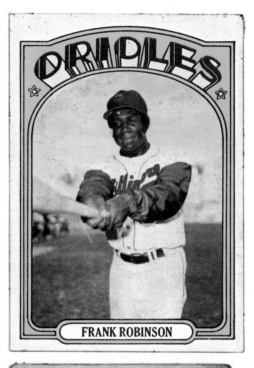

ORIOLES

FRANK ROBINSON

DICK GROAT

*shortstop* PITTSBURGH PIRATES

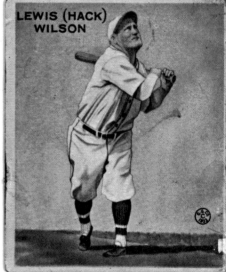

LEWIS (HACK)
WILSON

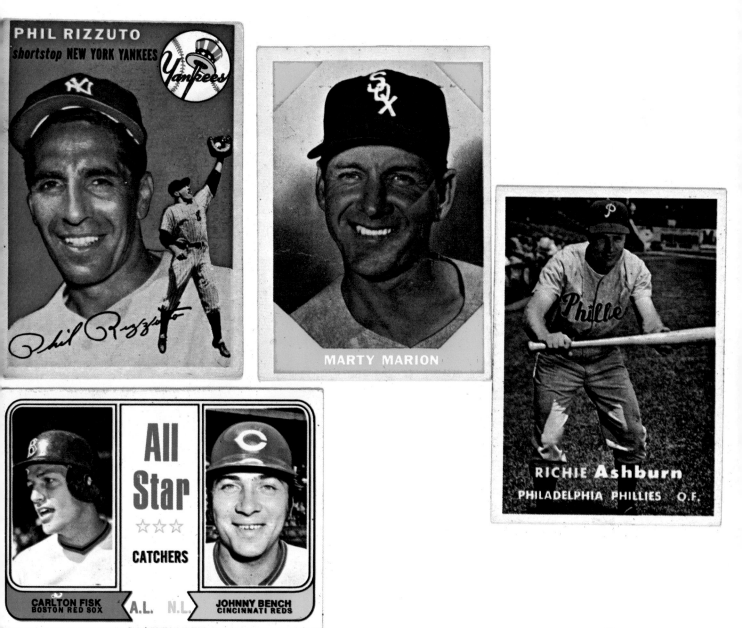

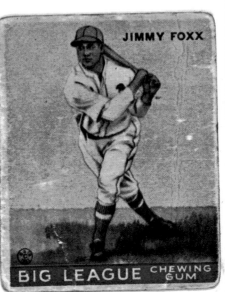

CHICAGO OUTFIELD

BILLY WILLIAMS CUBS

BABE RUTH SPECIAL BABE JOINS YANKS

FERGIE JENKINS CHICAGO CUBS PITCHER

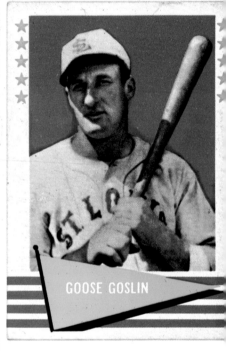

GOOSE GOSLIN

MICKEY COCHRANE

# Pee Wee Reese

S.S.-3rd B.    L. A. DODGERS

JOE MEDWICK

# CUBS

RON SANTO    **3rd base**

METS

P-COACH
**WARREN SPAHN**

ELSTON HOWARD
Catcher

New York Yankees

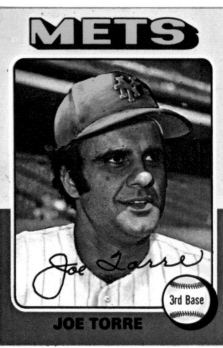

METS

JOE TORRE

3rd Base

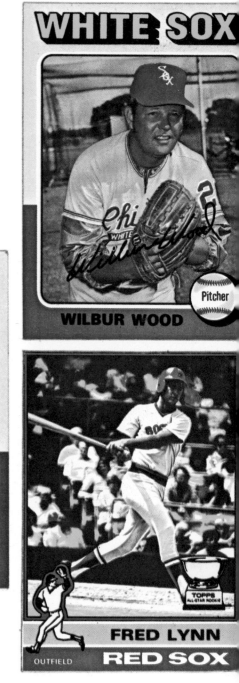

WHITE SOX

WILBUR WOOD

Pitcher

FRED LYNN

OUTFIELD

RED SOX

BOB FELLER
*pitcher* CLEVELAND INDIANS

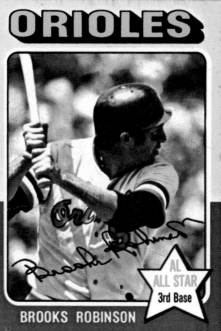

ORIOLES

BROOKS ROBINSON

AL ALL STAR
3rd Base

ROBERTO CLEMENTE
PITTSBURGH PIRATES

OUTFIELD

75

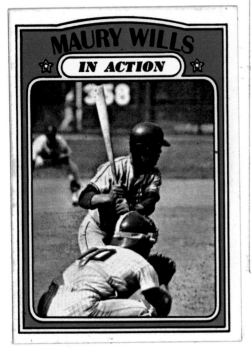

76

GEHRIG BENCHED
AFTER 2,130 GAMES

MANAGER
CASEY STENGEL

REDS

PETE ROSE

NL
ALL STAR
Outfield

ATHLETICS
jim hunter • pitcher

77

CUBS
leo durocher • manager

TOM SEAVER

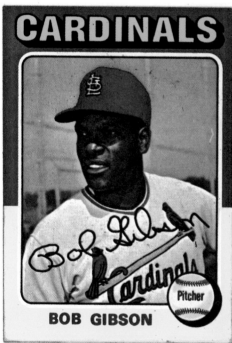

BOB GIBSON

CLETE
BOYER
N. Y. YANKEES        3B

MICKEY MANTLE
1st Base

YANKEES

MOSES

TWINS

Rod Carew | 2ND BASE

OAKLAND        PITCHER

VIDA
BLUE        A's

selling cards, or for auctions, there is interesting feature material supplied by collectors.

Editor Dischley regularly writes, "Collecting News," a gossip column of sorts on collectors. For example, "Rick Barudin found his third Wagner since opening his store about a year ago and shortly after acquiring it sold it to Joe and Karen Michalowicz. The reason it is mentioned here is that, unlike the usual Wagner, Joe and Karen's is a variation! A yellow background . . ." In his column, the editor has also been known to blacklist certain collectors "whose actions have continually hurt the hobby."

In an article on card collecting from California a contributor writes on the "Mirro-Krome" cards of 1959 which included two errors in their 12-card series.

Norm Larker's card had a picture of Joe Pignatano, and Clem Labine's card had a picture of Stan Williams.

In a piece on card variations a collector writes how Kellogg's 1975 3-D set has Catfish Hunter with two different backs — one has him in an Oakland Athletic cap with corresponding team insignia next to it. The other card has him in Yankee uniform.

And then there are the ads. Those who wish to sell cards indicate the type, specific card, condition (vg-very good, for instance), and price.

For example: "1938 Goudey Heads Up (vg-ex), Nos. 246, 247, 251, 258, 260 . . . ea. $7.50." Ads for auctions might read like this: "Bidding ends November 4 — E145 Cracker Jack (176 series) complete — 80% ex or better, 10% vg-ex, 5% vg, 5% gd, none f, 1 card p (No. 10). A beautiful set. Winner will also receive 7 cards (p-vg) from 144 series. Minimum bid $800."

For five cents per word, collectors may advertise at the back part of the publication. "Will pay $20 for 1959 Kahn's BB Dick Brodowski and No. 7 for 1958 Bond Bread. Phil Cavaretta." There are also other ads for sports nostalgia items, like: "For sale — baseball autographed by Lou Boudreau and nineteen of his Cleveland Indian players. Dated September 13, 1942."

Upcoming card conventions are also advertised. Information on price of table, admission, times, directions and even hotel rates are given.

The hobby's first bi-weekly, *Sports Collector's Digest*, published in Milan, Michigan, was begun in October, 1974. Subscription for a year costs $7.50.

Other publications include *Sports Fan*, a mimeographed bi-monthly published in Rosemont, Pennsylvania; the *Ballcard Collector's News*, a mimeographed monthly from Black River Falls, Wisconsin, and the *Ballcard Collector*, another mimeographed monthly from Corryton, Tennessee.

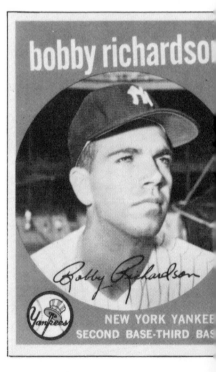

## Books

The granddaddy of baseball-card collector books is, of course, the *American Card Catalog*. A checklist for all types of cards from every era and manufacturer, the catalog is in its fourth revision by Woody Gelman. It is published by Nostalgia Press, Franklin Square, New York, and may be obtained from them.

*Sport Americana* is a baseball-card checklist from 1948 to the present. It includes all gum cards during the "modern era" of baseball-card collecting. It's available at hobby stores and conventions.

The *Baseball Card Alphabetical Handbook*, by Larry Fritsch and Bill Haber, is published by Helback Printing, Inc., of Amherst, Wisconsin. This book includes cards from Bowman, Fleers, Leaf, and Red Man (tobacco). It includes the player and the identifying number of his card each year.

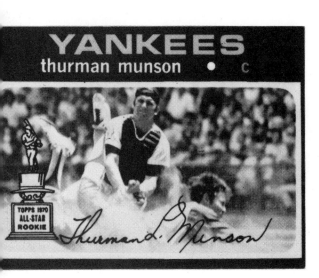

For example: Gus Bell — B53 BW-1 (Bowman, year 1953, black-and-white, No. 1); or Ted Williams — F59 1-80 (Fleers, in 1959, issued a whole series on Teddy).

One informative aspect of the book discloses how many cards have been issued on each player. Of the Topps cards, Hank Aaron and Willie Mays both have appeared on 22 cards (though Henry is now on 23), Harmon Killebrew has 20, Alvin Dark, Roberto Clemente, and Luis Aparicio have 19.

Similar to this book is the *Baseball Card Checklist*, which lists all gum cards numerically.

In addition to the books mentioned, other checklists come out on a regular basis by long-time collectors. As might be expected, when a good idea takes off, opportunists quickly climb upon the bandwagon.

## Auctions

The more sophisticated collector often buys cards through this method. Cards are advertised for auctioning in hobby publications, with a minimum bid usually indicated. Bids are then sent to the auctioneer. He then awards the card, or set of cards, to the highest bidder at a premium rate over the next highest bidder. For instance, if the highest bid is $75, and the next loftiest bid is only $25, the top bidder might receive the prize for only $26.

Of course, problems can arise. If two or more collectors bid extravagantly for the same card — with the intention of having their winning bid reduced substantially — they can get stuck.

Sports collecting clubs have been formed in many cities. They are considered an excellent way to meet other collectors. Active clubs include the Mid-Atlantic Sports Col-

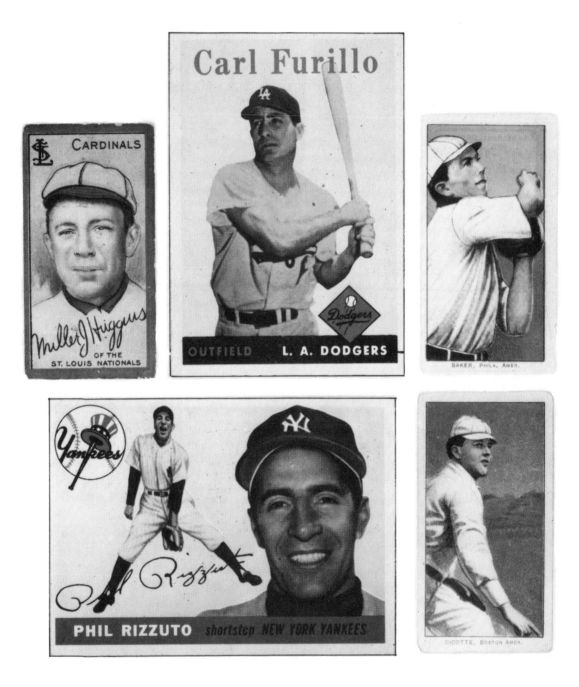

lectors Association, which meets monthly in Newcastle, Delaware, and the Southern California Sports Collectors Association, which has monthly meetings in Los Angeles. Other developing clubs are centered around Indianapolis, Buffalo, and several cities in Oregon.

One of the final things to know about collecting concerns procedures for storing and displaying cards. Big-time collectors recommend using index card-sized file cabinets. Cards may be filed numerically for each year and are immediately available simply by pulling out a cabinet drawer.

Since cards in fine condition are often worth twice as much as others, caution must be taken to keep them that way. Investing in a dehumidifier might be necessary to eliminate moisture which could cause cards to mildew. Who wants to purchase an expensive set of cards that turn into soggy pieces of cardboard?

# 8
# The Rare Ones

HARRY HEILMANN
OUTFIELD, DETROIT AMERICANS

SNODGRASS, N. Y. 'NAT'L

It would be a lot easier if things went something like this:

First collector: "Hey, how would you like to work a little trade? I'll give you my 1952 Topps Mickey Mantle, my 1949 Pacific Coast League stars, and a white-bordered Zack Wheat tobacco card for your 1954 Bowman series 88-96, a brown-bordered Roger Bresnahan, and the 1947 Tip-Top Bread series. What do you say?"

Second collector: "Let's see, now. Your cards are worth $250.88 and my cards go for $300.10. So if you throw in a check for $49.22, the deal is on."

So much for fantasy. Pricing baseball cards has become one of man's least-precise sciences. A card that might sell for $1 tomorrow might go for $20 next week. Similarly, one collector may be willing to pay $1,100 for a card that another bidder may be willing to spend only $110 for. Depending upon who's selling and who's buying, no price can be called too outlandish or considered too paltry.

M. BROWN, CHICAGO NAT'L

CRAWFORD, DETROIT

CUBS

John J. Evers
OF THE
CHICAGO NATIONALS

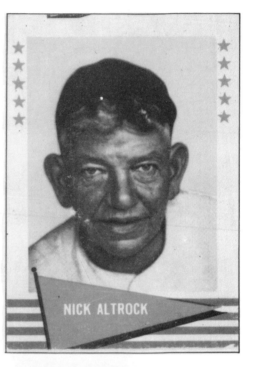

NICK ALTROCK

CUBS

Joe Tinker
OF THE
CHICAGO NATIONALS

"MEL" OTT

The *American Card Catalog* includes the values of all card sets from the early tobacco cards to the latest gum cards. Yet, these prices are really only the estimate of one man, Woody Gelman, based on the past reckoning of another man, Jefferson Burdick. Though it is based on past trades and comparative card costs, a card's value is still, as they say, at best a "ballpark fig- ure." Additionally, the catalog does not take into account the value of certain rare cards and variation cards.

In the last few years, the value of the superstar has skyrocketed. From Sweet Caporal to Topps, the card manufacturers have annually printed equal amounts of cards for the .350 hitter, the 20-game win- ner, the .245 hitter, and the five-game win-

BABE RUTH SPECIAL

BABE AND MGR. HUGGINS

ner. So, unlike most other times when supply and demand determine ultimate card value, the accent in this instance is simply on demand. In 1955, Topps issued the same number of Mickey Mantle cards as Leo Kiely cards.

Of the superstars, Babe Ruth demands the highest trade value, followed by Lou Gehrig, Joe DiMaggio, Ted Williams, Mickey Mantle, Hank Aaron, Willie Mays, Roberto Clemente, and Sandy Koufax.

Variations, or error cards, usually are more valuable than other cards from the same year and company. Variations can be extreme (as the chapter on goofs indicates) or minute. It can be anything from a color change to an incorrect back to a wrong face.

Gum card variations go back as far as 1949, when Bowman issued only a half dozen of its 116-card series with the written name on the back. In the following year, the company omitted printing the final line, "1950 Bowman Gum, Inc., Phil., Pa., U.S.A." on the backs of about one-third of their entire series. In 1955, the year the company went out of business, there were a number of variations. The cards of brothers Frank and Milt Bolling (No. 48 and No. 204) had the backs transposed. Card No. 101 had an Ernie Johnson front and a Don Johnson back. Harvey Kuenn's card had his name spelled "Kueen" on the back. The card of Erv Palica was printed with and without the last line, "Sent to Baltimore when Preacher Roe retired."

The 1948 Leaf Cards issued its No. 102 card of Gene Hermanski with and without the "i." (They wanted to be sure to get it right!) Card No. 136 of Cliff Aberson pictured him with a full sleeve on his left arm on some cards and a half-sleeve (on the same arm) on others.

Topps, of course, also has its corner on the variation market. In 1961, there were two No. 643's issued — pitcher Jack Fisher and the Milwaukee Braves team. In 1962, for some reason, the company was so enamored with Yankee relief pitcher Hal Reniff that they offered him as No. 139 twice (in different positions) and as No. 159. No superstar ever received such treatment.

A 1966 checklist listed both Warren Spahn and Bill Henry as No. 115. In 1967, Bob Priddy is a Giant on the front and a Senator on the back. Checklist No. 454 has two different Juan Marichals pictured, one with one ear and one with two ears. A 1969 checklist calls No. 161 John Purdin in some, Jim Purdin in others. And the list goes on.

Throughout the years, for both known and unknown reasons, cards of certain players have acquired a rating of "rare." Collector Gar Miller includes the following players as coming under this heading:

Honus Wagner and Eddie Plank, the rarest, as mentioned earlier; a .250ish outfielder from St. Louis named Ray Demitt; Sherwood Magie of the Philadelphia team; William O'Hara of St. Louis, who played only two major-league seasons; pitcher Adrian Joss of Cleveland; Bugs Raymond, a New York Giant pitcher; John Rowan, an under-.500 hurler who was traded five times in six years; Cotton Turner, who put in a long line of service with the Indians; and Grover Cleveland Lowdermilk (that's the truth), whose named surpassed his playing ability with a multitude of teams. All these cards were issued prior to World War I.

Among the highly sought-after gum cards are Napoleon Lajoie (No. 106 in 1934) and Nos. 109-110 in set R330, and No. 96 in R320.

Jim Konstanty, Robin Roberts, and Eddie Stanky are hard to get in the 1950 Current All-Star issue; Dodgers Gino Cimoli and Duke Snider in the 1958 Bell Brand series; Mario Candini, a Washington Sen-

"KIKI" CUYLER

A. LEAGUE 1966 HOME RUN LEADERS

FRANK ROBINSON
BALTIMORE ORIOLES

HARMON KILLEBREW
MINNESOTA TWINS

BOOG POWELL
BALTIMORE ORIOLES

PAUL DERRINGER

ator pitcher, Giant pitcher Buddy Kerr, Pirate hurler Louis Tost, knock-around pitcher Jim Wilson, and Boston moundsman Pinky Woods of the 1949 Remar cards; No. 66, Ted Williams, in the 1954 Bowman; Stan Musial in 1954 Red Heart; Ken Boyer in 1959 Topps; Joe Gibbon and Vic Power in 1962 Kahn's; the first three series in 1955 Johnston Cookies; Bob Shaw and Mel Roach in 1962 Post Cereal; Babe Ruth in Yeungling's; Luke Easter in the 1958 Bond Bread; No. 68 in Fleer's Ted Williams series of 1959; and Joe Adcock of 1963 Fleer's.

According to collector Irving Lerner, several other cards are highly valued for different reasons. Bowman's 1948 card of American League third baseman George Kell, for example, was one Lerner paid $50 for. "The players revolted that year," said Lerner. "They didn't get paid for appearing on the cards. Forty-nine of the players didn't care and 49 wanted money or you had to recall their cards. Kell's card was one of those recalled; therefore, a rarity."

Another card that would be worth a lot,

if it exists, is the 1958 card of Phillie first baseman Ed Bouchee. Bouchee is listed as No. 145 that year, but the printing of his card was stopped when he was charged with a morals offense early that year. Topps is almost positive none got out, but . . .

Due to poor distribution, Topps cards 311-407 of the 1952 series didn't make it to most outlets. The company destroyed many of the cards when the season ended. Today, these cards have extra value.

Topp's 1955 supplementary Double Header series is also worth more. Each card has a value of $1.50-$2.00 at most conventions.

Once again, it must be pointed out that fixing a price on any card or series is just some person's estimate, and a transient guess at best. The only reason for giving prices here is to show comparative values.

In the *American Card Catalog*, as well as in auctions and sales, key letters indicate a particular type of card. Numbers are affixed to indicate sub-divisions.

The 1910 era tobacco cards are given the letter "T," as in T200, T201, etc.; the gum

cards are R318, R319, etc.; bakery cards are D315, D317, etc.; the caramel and early candy cards are E90, E92; the oil- and gas-company cards are U010, U011; cards from other foods are F151, F153.

Considered the most expensive of the tobacco series are the T200 cards, which are the Fatima cards issued in 1913. The 16-card set is valued at approximately $6 per card. T202, which are Hassan Triple Folders issued in 1912, go for about $4 each. There were 76 cards in that series. A much larger series, like the T206 White Border cards which were issued in 1910 and included 523 small-sized cards, are valued at only about 50¢ each.

The 24 Play Ball cards issued by DeLong Gum in 1933, R333, each have a value of about $20. The 1938 Goudey Heads-Up cards — R323, and 48 in number — go for $4 each. National Chicle's Batter-Up Series in the 1930's, R318, is evaluated at $4 for each card under No. 80; twice as much for higher numbers. The Philadelphia Gum cards of 1939, R334, are worth about $1.50 for Nos. 1-116; $3 for higher numbers.

The most coveted set of modern gum cards are considered to be the Topps 1950 Current Stars series, valued at $20 apiece. The 1952 Topps cards over No. 310 bring about $8 each. All Topps cards are listed as R414.

The Bowman cards treasured most are the R406, the 1949 Pacific Coast League cards. Each of the 36 cards are valued at $10. The Fleer's cards are considered to be worth little more than 15¢ or 20¢ a shot. Excluding superstars, cards of the 1960's bring about 8¢ apiece. Early 1970 cards are worth no more than 4¢ each.

Some of the regional cards are valued quite highly. 36 Drake's Cookies cards, D358, issued in 1950, bring about $8 today. The 1946 Remar Bread cards issued in California, D315, are worth about $5. The Glendale Meats Detroit Tigers cards of 1953, F151, and the 1953-55 Hunter's Wieners cards of the St. Louis Cardinals, F153, each bring as much as $15. The 1958 Bell Brand Dodgers, F339, are about $6, and the 1954 Dan-Dee Chips, F342, are valued at about $10 for each of its 29 cards.

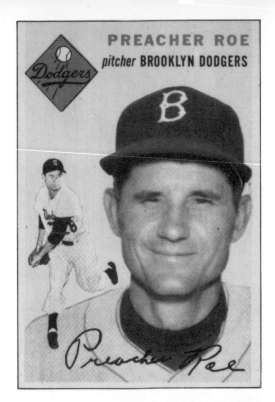

In comparison, the 1954 Red Heart Dog Food, F156, and 1958 Hires Root Beer cards, F211, are only worth about 50¢.

Any Babe Ruth or Lou Gehrig gum or candy card is evaluated at a minimum of $20, if in mint condition. Topps' 1952 Mickey Mantle (No. 311) card (the year of distribution problems), which some have paid $100 for, is considered that company's most valued single card.

In any case, cards that might turn up in the attic, an old shoe box, a rented dresser, or in your ancient confirmation pants, may be worth a lot more than you thought. Then, again, you might only be able to bargain for a fast 50¢. There's no guarantee that the value of a card will increase with time. Consider it more like a stock; depending on the times, it could be worth a mint — gold or chocolate.

# 9

# A Trip to the Factory

Duryea is only a small dot on the state map, not unlike any small community in northeastern Pennsylvania. The narrow streets are lined with small stores, diners, gas stations, and churches. Evidence of strip mining abounds in the distance.

Every day, a station wagon makes the trip from the Brooklyn executive and marketing offices of Topps Chewing Gum, Inc. to its Duryea plant. The route is a fairly direct one—Interstate Highway 80 through relatively flat land in New Jersey, then past more mountainous country and the Delaware Water Gap in Pennsylvania, through the small town of Avoca, over its railroad tracks, and into Duryea, home of some 6,000 people.

The factory is a white spick-and-span building atop a hill. Sharing the hill and a view of the West Mountains is the plant of the Schott Optical Company.

Topps moved part of their operation to Duryea in October, 1965. Things were too hectic back in Brooklyn. The executive types and the manufacturing types both needed some breathing room.

Though visiting the plant would make an ideal field trip for schoolchildren, there are no school buses in the parking lot. For that matter, there are few cars parked here that do not belong to Topps employees.

Topps does not encourage visitors. In fact, the company takes a somewhat paranoid view of visitors entering their plant. This means no local townspeople, no curiosity seekers, no snoopy reporters.

With the manufacture of gum and candy products and the cutting, collating, and packaging of cards done here, Topps fears the presence of industrial spies, those men in trench coats and dark glasses who might obtain the secret of their production line. Topps utilizes special machinery, and doesn't want to risk having the competition gain knowledge of their techniques.

Once inside — for those who pass the screening test — there is no mistaking one's location. A large table in the middle of the reception room, with sunken pockets along its borders, is filled to the brim with Bazooka Gum. Decorations on the wall are all in salute to father — Topps Chewing Gum.

The personnel offices are similarly adorned. There is a blow-up of Charles Shulz's comic-strip character, Charlie Brown, frustrated as usual because he has just spent $5 in search of a card of his favorite baseball player, Joe Shlabotnik, without luck. Lucy Van Pelt, his nemesis, of course, finds Joe in her first pack. Also pictured on the wall is another Joe — Joe Garagiola. The sports celebrity emceed Topps' major-league bubble gum blow-off contest, and endeared himself to the company. He has also visited here.

In any travel through the factory, workers and visitors alike are given a cafeteria-style hat or a golf hat to wear, a health pre-caution — to keep loose hair from getting into the gum.

The aroma of sweet, tangy gum is the first thing to greet one's nostrils. And then one sees rows and rows of Big Mouth and Gold Rush and Garbage Candy and gumballs and Bazooka. Confectionery heaven! So this is how that wicked witch lured Hansel and Gretel!

Big vats and special gum-shaping and wrapping machines fill most of the plant. Employees pack and wrap the product as it falls from machines. Mechanical assembly lines also pitch in.

Set off in a corner is the real reason for the visit — the cutting, collating and wrapping of baseball cards. A sign on the wall directs how the cards should be cut. You don't want to nip off Don Gullett's fingers or Dave Kingman's bat, so there are special guidelines. Machines are adjusted so that the cuts are perfect.

The cutting machines are each operated by a woman who feeds solid sheets of baseball cards (132 cards to a sheet) into it. The machine devours the sheet and spits out individual cards. Each card must now stand on its own.

Another woman operates a collating machine, a gizmo not unlike a windmill that separates cards with the same faces from each other. The cards are then wrapped and stuffed into boxes.

The cards, and the gum, are then shipped to the warehouse. Compared to the *click-clack* of the gum and card machines, the storage rooms are like morgues. The only sound is that of the occasional passing of a crane-like vehicle moving crates of baseball cards and bubble-gum treats. All of the big boxes have tickets on them, indicating a destination — Baltimore, Boston, Endicott, Little Rock, Santa Ana. . . .

This is the last stop on the Topps trail.

JOE BLACK
pitcher BROOKLYN DODGERS

HANK AARON SPECIAL

1970   1971
1972   1973

HANK AARON

HANK AARON
ATLANTA BRAVES

RED SOX

CARL YASTRZEMSKI   of

nellie fox

SOX

CHICAGO WHITE SOX
SECOND BASE

Harvey Kuenn

OUTFIELD   DETROIT TIGERS

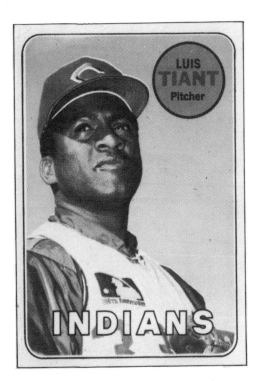

Yet, a visitor cannot help but note a dedication when leaving. A plaque reads: "This building is dedicated to the citizens of Scranton, Pittston, Wilkes-Barre and the other nearby communities of northeast Pennsylvania. Their gracious welcome, their warm cooperation, and their continued friendly spirit have set a high standard of community endeavor."

This is not merely an idle inscription.

Topps Chewing Gum has been a major boost to the local economy that has been plagued by mine shutdowns and floods in recent years. The factory employs some 1,100 people from the area who participate in the production and distribution of gum, candy, and millions of cards daily.

How do they like it? As one worker declared, "Where else can you make money for doing kids' stuff?"

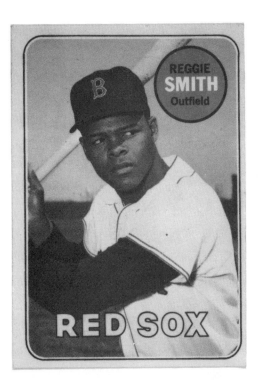

# 10
# The Games They Play

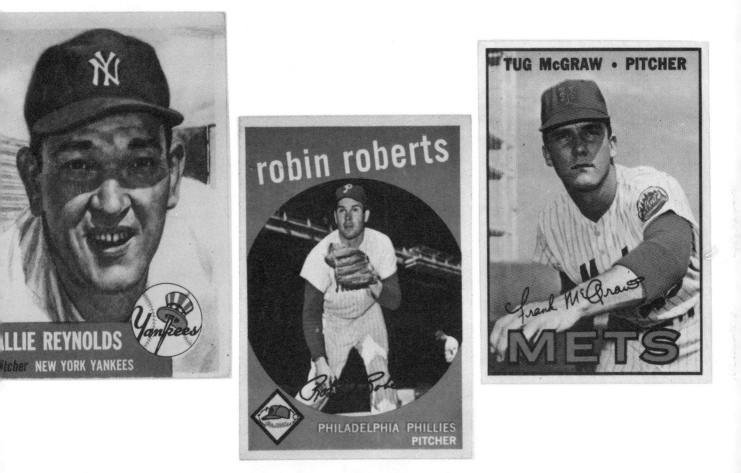

It happens every spring while the major-league pitchers and swatters are still down south grooving their arms or their bats. It's a bit of news that passes through the neighborhood as quickly as the sound of Johnny's mother punishing Johnny for not doing his homework. And it has been around ever since there have been boys and girls in the 20th century.

The call of the baseball card is heard each March throughout the towns and cities of America. The first pack of baseball cards that lands at Old Man Riley's candy store in Des Moines or at Milton & Ethel's Luncheonette in the Bronx heralds the arrival of the new season — not spring, or even baseball season, but baseball-card season.

World Series popularity notwithstanding, baseball is no longer America's No. 1 sport. The game has slipped a rung or two on the sporting ladder behind football, and perhaps basketball. Yet, according to the people at Topps, one-quarter of a billion baseball cards are sold annually, and that number continues to rise every year. Baseball cards still are bought twice as hungrily as football or basketball or hockey cards.

According to Topps' Sy Berger, youngsters storm the neighborhood candy stores for baseball cards for three major reasons: "First, there is the identification. The baseball player is typical of the man walking down the street, unlike the football player who is a very big man, or the basketball player who is a very tall man. With a baseball player, he can see himself. He can identify. In addition, because of the game's slow pace, the youngster has the opportunity to learn to imitate baseball players — to hold his bat like Willie Mays, crouch like Stan Musial, or spread his feet like Joe DiMaggio. And he can familiarize himself with the facts about the players. It's all within his grasp."

As much as the initial curiosity a youngster has in seeing how his favorite players look this season, the opening of the baseball-card season also means the advent of "flipping." Every poor flipper who has seen his investments plummet in past seasons figures hopefully that this is the year his fortunes will change. The successful flipper sees the new year as an opportunity to take on some new marks in the neighborhood flipping wars.

Flippers who have a steady income of cards usually will flip their duplicates and their .195 hitters. The less fortunate youngsters, of course, must do battle with their front-liners. In either case, the game of flipping has caused more black eyes and bloodied noses than any touch football game. "Take my only Hank Aaron card, will you? You can have my little brother, instead!"

There are many flipping games, some done in sedentary position, some done kneeling or standing. Following are the rules and an assessment of some of the more popular games that can sink a fortune or make one wealthy.

## Colors

Colors, as in Teams and Positions, is a game where two or more players passively

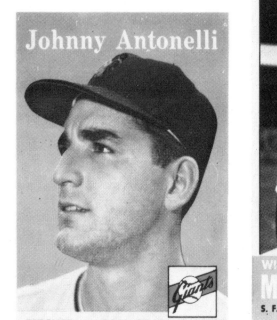

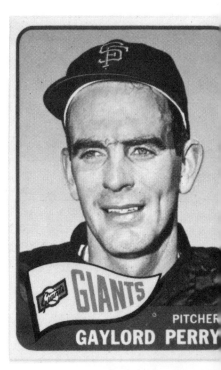

sit next to each other and dole out their fortunes in rapid-fire succession. Some flipping purists won't even consider Colors a part of the flipping spectrum, because of the lack of skill involved. This is an understatement — the game is entirely a matter of luck. The player throwing the first card announces the game, as in poker. He might say, "Colors five times," which means that the color on the bottom of the card (there are usually a half-dozen different colors) must be matched by a player five times.

When playing with more than two people, Teams is the game where a player must worry about collaboration by his foes. Since it is more difficult to match Astros with Astros or Dodgers with Dodgers than it is to match green with green or red with red, one match usually signals victory and the winning of all the cards in the pile. Two hustlers can conceivably arrange their cards beforehand so that after a dozen or so throws, they come up with a team match.

Other varieties of these games are Names, which is matching first names, Initials, or Dates, which is the year of the player's birth found on the back of his card.

## Topsies

Topsies is basically a city game, simply because it is usually played against an apartment house stoop. The idea of the game is to get a card to land atop a card that is already in the pot. As in Colors, one player usually decrees beforehand the number of "topsies" that win.

Another rule which must be predetermined to be in effect is whether or not "tippies" are valid. By saying "Tippies allowed," a card that winds up barely touching another card's corner is considered a "topsy."

The reason for the stoop is that almost all flippers worthy of the name ricochet cards off the stoop. Gripping a card with forefinger against the outside corner, thumb on top and the other three fingers on the bottom, a player will eye a card near the stoop. By bouncing a card off the stoop with proper velocity, he hopes to top the card.

A variation of Topsies is Undertopsies, which means flipping a card *under* a card already flipped. This is a much more diffi-

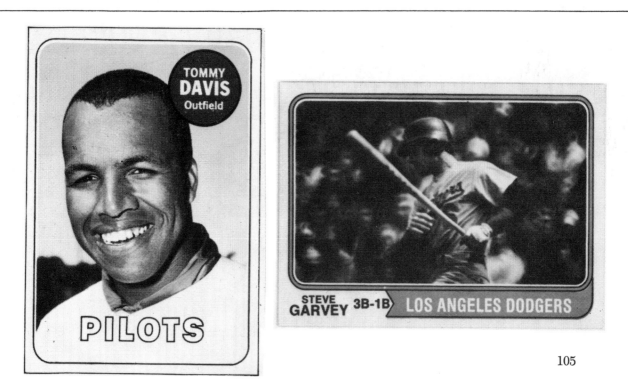

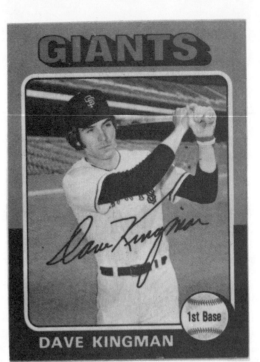

GIANTS

DAVE KINGMAN

1st Base

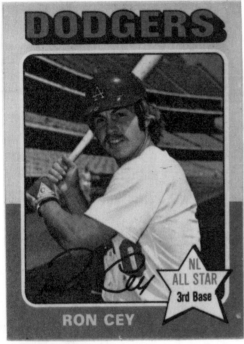

DODGERS

NL ALL STAR
3rd Base

RON CEY

CLAUDE OSTEEN
CINCINNATI REDS        PITCHER

ROYALS

JOHN MAYBERRY

1st Base

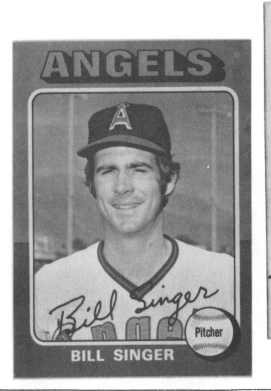

cult game. Another game is Off the Wall, where the object is to top cards by simply dropping cards off a wall. This is basically for younger children because of the relative ease of the game. It is to Topsies what training wheels are to a racing bike.

## Scaling

Scaling is also known as Farthees, a game where the farthest distance a card is flipped determines the winner. Since not too many cards are gambled in this game

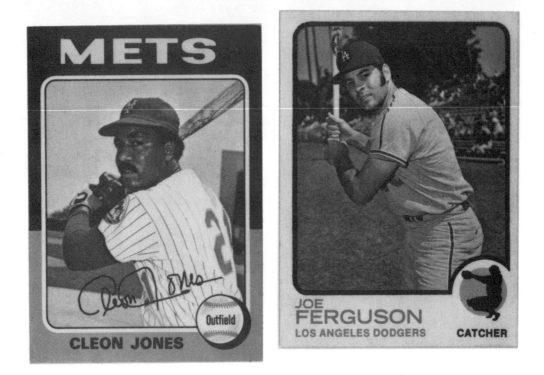

(although the house rule can be that the farthest out of ten cards wins), this is not one of the more popular games. Stakes, not skill, usually result in popularity.

## Knock Down the Leaner

Knock Down the Leaner, and its side-kick, Make a Leaner, are two games that combine skill and high stakes. Again, both games are won by someone who accomplishes the specific feat.

In Knock Down the Leaner, several cards are usually leaned vertically or horizontally (depending on the rules) against a wall or stoop. The competitors then pace off a set distance from which to shoot.

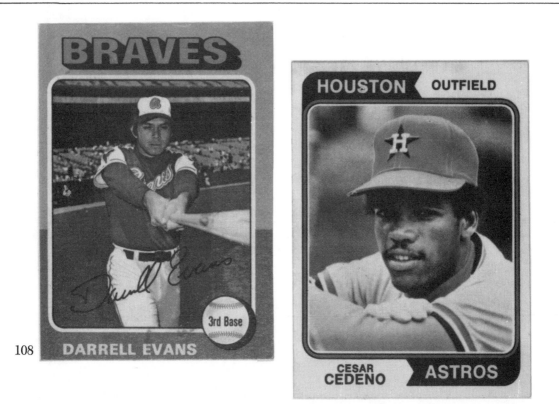

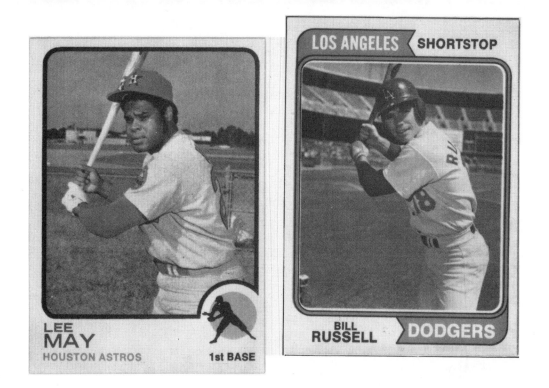

Position is important here, sometimes by choice or rule. The flipper can either stand, squat, sit, or lie down. Unless there are rules to the contrary, the player who squats (or leans his knees against the floor) is in the best position to knock down leaners.

Making a Leaner is a bit more difficult. Again, the backdrop is a stoop or a wall. As the name implies, flippers attempt to throw a card that will lean or stand up against the backdrop. Instead of using the normal flipping grip (as explained under Topsies and used for Knock Down the Leaner and scaling), the flippers slide the card against the surface, which is usually smooth. (A rough surface makes this game even more difficult.) The flipper puts four fingers on top of the card (all but the

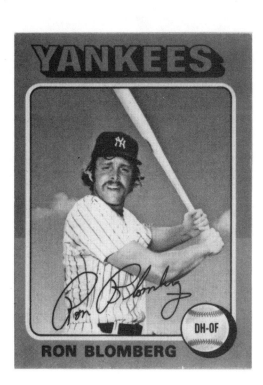

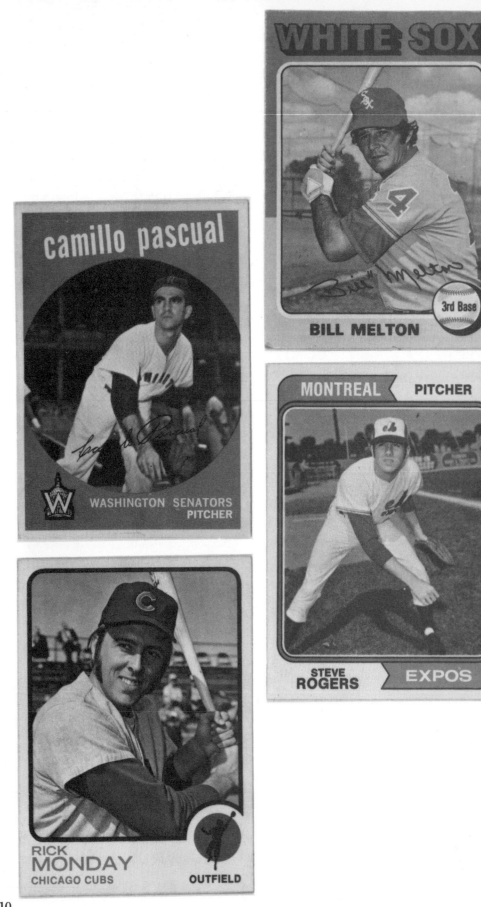